Life Skills

Life Skills

Taking Charge of Your Personal and
Professional Growth

Richard J. Leider

Pfeiffer
& COMPANY

Amsterdam • Johannesburg • London
San Diego • Sydney • Toronto

Contents

Preface

In searching for a graphic concept that symbolizes the content and purpose of *Life Skills*, we came upon the Chambered Nautilus (Nautilus pompilius). We chose this unique and beautiful creature because it possesses a combination of characteristics that we as human beings could do well to cultivate.

- **CONTINUED GROWTH.** Throughout its life, the Nautilus continually grows, adding new chambers, new dimensions to its life and structure.

- **ADAPTABILITY.** The Nautilus easily adjusts to extremes of pressure by changing the water and air pressure in its chambers. It can live at immense depths.

- **DURABILITY.** The Nautilus has survived and thrived for millions of years in the face of profound changes in the world around it.

- **DISTINCTIVENESS.** Inside and out, the Nautilus presents an appearance all its own: outside, a creamy white shell and wavy brown lines; inside, a lining of mother-of-pearl.

- **RARITY.** The Chambered Nautilus is also rare—almost as rare, perhaps, as those individuals who devote the necessary time and effort to really taking charge of their lives.

In the months and years to come, will you adapt to your environment as well as the Chambered Nautilus docs to its? We hope this book will be a useful motivator and guide in helping you achieve your goals.

Introduction

The Objective

> "Most of us never
> learned about change
> except through
> trial-and-error
> experience. But
> experience is not
> enough today.
> We need to take
> charge of change."

The aim of the *Life Skills* program is to empower you to significantly increase your change management skills and your performance capability. With today's accelerating rate of change, everybody needs to know how to manage change in order to survive. The people who prosper during the next decade will be those with the ability to respond to change quickly and effectively. This means individuals will need a simple, clear model to plan and institute personal change.

Individuals today have to deal with three changing environments. Waves of change sweep across the globe, and you must learn to interpret these changes accurately. The second change is the environment of the organizations you work for and with.

Many of us do not respond to the same leadership and incentives as employees of a few years ago. The third aspect of the changing environment is the impact on your personal life. The events of the past three decades have basically transformed the relationships among individuals, organizations, and families. Today, it is more difficult than ever to make decisions about life and career tradeoffs.

Change is difficult. People often avoid change. Most never learned about change except through trial-and-error experience. But experience is not enough today. You need to *take charge* of change.

Life Skills was written to help individuals respond to the challenge of today's rapid change. As a toolbook it offers strategies for *understanding* the past, *managing* the present, and *creating* the future. To the degree this process is widely shared, an organization becomes empowered to act on its vision and align its members behind this vision.

The Questions

There is no one right change formula or strategy. Each of you must define your own. Yet, regardless of your unique priorities and needs, during times of change we all ask questions like those below:

1. Who am I?
2. Why am I here?
3. Where am I going?
4. How will I get there?
5. What are my priorities?
6. What's the new vision?
7. Will I have a place in it?
8. Will I fit?
9. What do I need to learn?
10. How do I maintain control?
11. What are my tradeoffs?
12. What will I need to give up?
13. Where do I grow from here?

How individuals, organizations, and families deal with these questions has changed radically over the past thirty years.

The Answers

The outcomes of the *Life Skills* process are highly individualized. It can teach you how to

- Understand the change process.
- Use personal strategies to manage and create change effectively.
- View organizational changes as opportunties, not threats.
- Manage your own feelings, motivations, and quality-of-life satisfaction.
- Develop your own value-based, purpose-centered vision.
- Renew your energy.
- Improve time and self-management skills.

The Life Skills Process

The *Life Skills* process presents key concepts of change and self-management in a personal action plan. It offers insights, along with tools you'll be able to implement immediately. The process not only creates awareness but also gives you the information needed to design a personal growth plan to enhance job performance and personal life effectiveness.

The *Life Skills* process is a framework that will help you ask the right questions and put a plan together that addresses the whole you: work, family, leisure, health, finances, and spiritual life. The process is designed to stimulate your understanding of the process of growth and to increase your change management skills. It presents the premise that increased "change vitality" is a desirable and achievable goal for both individuals and organizations. This book provides the tools for analyzing how you grow and change and the techniques for prioritizing what you want from work and life.

The Content

The model of change and growth used in *Life Skills* is based on observations and studies of highly effective people.

Life Skills focuses on four "learnings":
(1) How to deal with change
(2) How to discover purpose
(3) How to create a personal vision
(4) How to balance daily priorities and tradeoffs.

1. Deal With Change

All of us, to varying extents, are limited by our fears—of criticism, of rejection, of betrayal, of failure, of success. We lack trust in ourselves. We often doubt our own good judgment in the face of contrary opinions from others. Also, we often lack the trust in others that is necessary to create a high-performing team or organization. Fear is a choice. We can "rescript" ourselves to reduce fear and embrace change.

2. Discover Purpose

Discovering a sense of purpose is crucial to making a difference in our work and our lives. Self-knowledge, however, does not come easy. Some people, manage to travel quite happily through life without ever knowing themselves. Whether because of luck, or good intuitive timing, they do very well. However, even those people, to their dismay, wake up at some point asking, "Who am I?" "Why am I here?" "Where am I going?" The best leadership today is based on fostering a guiding purpose in others and clarifying the organization's purpose.

3. Create a Personal Vision

A clear vision sets in motion the factors and forces to create the future. A familiar example is the athlete whose performance is limited by an invisible barrier, as the four-minute mile once was. With a clear vision that breaks through previous limits, the athlete reprograms the belief system and consequently achieves superior performance. This power of creating a vision is critical to individuals and organizations today.

4. Track Daily Priorities

Life Skills helps you develop a solid growth plan that accommodates change, yet endures. You assemble a base of information about yourself in a logically organized, summarized plan, for ready referral whenever you need it.

Your Life Growth Plan, when used consistently, will have a profound and lasting impact. The art of self-leadership can be learned like any other skill.

The Principles

The principles aren't subtle or complex, but they cover the core aspects of growth and self-management. The principles are as follows:

1. *Time*
You must understand your real priorities and tradeoffs or you risk wasting your most valuable currency—time.

2. *Values*
The quality and depth of your self-worth is a key indicator; you must be clear about your values because they reveal who you really are.

3. *Vitality*
Living with vitality is the bottom line; vitality comes from integrity and integrity comes from one simple act: keeping the promises you make to yourself.

4. *Purpose*
Living and working from a clear sense of purpose creates enduring meaning and satisfaction.

5. *Career*
To be fulfilled in your work, it is crucial to connect talents with interests and passions in an environment that fits your values.

6. *Spirituality*
Living from a clear sense of purpose requires making consistent contact with a power greater than yourself.

7. *Health*
The key to health is doing little things consistently; life energy is built or destroyed by many individual actions that become your pattern.

8. *Talents*
Recognize your talents to discover if you are fully using them. You become energized when your talents and work align.

9. *Relationships*
Establish relationship and support systems that can carry you through the various transitions of work/life.

10. *Money*
Decide by which criteria you want to measure success.

Change, though often a struggle, can be an opportunity to grow, to strengthen vision, and to enhance performance. If you understand and apply the *Life Skills* principles, you can experience change as growth.

The Challenge

I

Inner Kill

The most insatiable killer in America is not heart disease, cancer, or alcohol. It's "Inner Kill." Inner Kill is the art of dying without knowing it. It's when routine living seems to have dulled your emotions. It's feeling like you're coping without being fully alive.

Inner Kill is not growing. It's taking the safe way. Always covering for yourself instead of taking risks. It's reacting, instead of thinking. It's giving up control of your life to whatever or whomever is around you. Inner Kill is the death of self-respect.

You have Inner Kill when you

• Avoid decisions.

• Daydream about early retirement.

• Talk a lot about what you're going to do, but do nothing.

- Lay awake nights, sleepwalk by day.
- Experience unusual irritability as the norm.
- Talk to friends about the same things week after week.

Inner Kill is the chief symptom of people who are afraid to live. Perhaps the fact of life most conducive to taking charge is an honest awareness and acceptance of death. Death is the greatest of life's teachers. It is those who are afraid to live who fear it most.

Death has no secrets. If you are willing to look, it constantly makes its presence known. It is everywhere, even in organizations. When one is taking charge as a person, death is less of a threat. Rather, it serves as life's greatest teacher. It reminds you that it is not always the other person who dies. Death tells you to live now, in the moment. Every day is new. Every moment is fresh. Time is yours, given freely to spend wisely or to squander idly, but never to be taken for granted. Perhaps the most irresponsible phrase in the English language is "I should have."

Death is too often denied. Understanding death as another aspect of the change cycle, allows you to approach change differently and give value to each life encounter, knowing that it will never occur again. In each of these moments you'll be taking charge. The wise discover death to be an astute teacher and make it a lifelong ally.

Most larger businesses require their employees to do annual planning and budgeting. People are advised to review their health and finances annually or every two years. Isn't it even more important to regularly step back and reassess one's career and life?

At different times in life you take stock. You try to be reasonable, to compare what you have (and could lose) with "greener pasture" fantasies. You try to make rational decisions about the status quo or changing it.

But there are points in your life and career when work priorities conflict with personal priorities or most desired lifestyle. It's perplexing trying to determine whether life goals should be modified to accommodate your career, or vice versa. The easiest course is often to stick with the status quo, which often leads us to "Inner Kill."

Life Skills is based on the following assumptions:

1. Life is change.
2. All change is self-change.
3. Self-change requires risk-taking.
4. Lack of risk-taking results in "Inner Kill."
5. Risk-taking is emotional.
6. With emotions there are two choices:
   - Expression
   - Depression
7. Taking charge involves sharpening the skills of daily reflection and expression.

In studies of the life satisfaction of many people, the same theme repeats itself: what most people want out of life, more than anything else, is the opportunity to grow and to have choices. The greatest tragedy in life is to stop growing and to cease exercising choices.

Studies of older adults reporting high well-being in their sixties, seventies and eighties show that their lives involved conscious personal risks. They stepped outside their "comfort zones" on to their "growth edge."

Living at risk, on one's growth edge, is the opposite of Inner Kill. Life is seen as an error-making and an error-correcting process. You learn; your problems become your teachers. As Richard Bach in his book *Illusions* stated, "Every tragedy has a gift for you in its hands."

It's hard sometimes to accept the gift. It's normal to experience periods when you are depressed, frustrated, and down on yourself. Studies of older adults who have effectively moved through normal periods of life's ups and downs point to the Four Learnings identified in the Introduction.

1. Deal With Change
They had a support system to turn to in difficult times.

2. Discover Purpose
They had a commitment to growing and shaping that growth, to make a difference.

3. Create a Personal Vision
They had the ability to periodically reflect on their lives.

4. Track Daily Priorities
They were willing to set goals and regularly track their progress.

"The best place to find a helping hand," it has been said, "is at the end of your arm." Your willingness to complete the activities in this book decreases your likelihood of Inner Kill.

13

Will You Miss Your Wake-Up Call?

Everyone knows the phenomenon of being more or less awake on different days. At different times in life, your talents are slumbering and the interests of the day don't seem to call forth your energies.

Awakening to your priorities, you often realize that you've been asleep, drifting off into postponement: "When I get it all together in the future, then I'll start living. Then, all of a sudden, you wake up to find that, as Sam Levinson puts it, "When I finally got the means to an end, they moved the ends further apart."

Sooner or later it happens to most of us. You get a "wake-up call."

Wake-up calls are similar to those events—those "moments of truth" or revelations—we all occasionally experience. These calls can act as catalysts to change and to decision making. They may be startling, or one morning you may wake up knowing you can't continue in the same way. You must act!

Life is a series of challenges—highs and lows. Anyone can handle the high points. The big moments take care of themselves. It's the valleys and plateaus, the postponements, that you need to learn to handle. Nothing could be more normal than these plateaus and valleys;

they are inevitable parts of human existence. But what is not normal is the way in which you cope with them.

Taking charge calls for both reflection and expression. You wouldn't expect a person to design a complex building without a blueprint, or after just a week-long seminar in architecture. Yet often you expect to be a different person—awake, perhaps—from just reading a book like this. It's one thing to understand the fundamentals of planning; it's another to change habits and stay awake!

You need to wake up your potentials. But, how? How can you escape this sleep?

Often, you can't awaken by yourself. You must be looked after by people who aren't asleep or who don't fall asleep as easily as you do. You must find people and ask them to wake you up and not to allow you to fall asleep again.

Who awakens you? Who gives you that periodic wake-up call to the possibilities inherent in your life and work?

A good place to start with a quality-of-life exploration is at its roots, by asking, "Why do I get up in the morning?" Repeat the question several times aloud. Are you comfortable with your answer?

In a busy life, reasons for getting up in the morning often become blurred. You're a train passenger who doesn't know where the train is or where it's going. Often you're surprised at where it takes you and where it stops, but you stay on for the ride. Achieving a clearer life vision often requires that you change direction or destination, or prepare for unexpected stops or detours. Don't get locked into one track if you don't want to be. There are switches you can throw throughout your life.

We've divided "life" into eight stages. These stages are like the chambers of the nautilus. In each chamber the developing individual confronts new growth challenges—wake-up calls—and takes on new tasks in response to those calls.

We've laid the stages out on the next pages, pointing out the challenges that must be handled as you grow from stage to stage.

The Life Chambers activity gives you an opportunity to gain a thought-stimulating overview of where you've been during your life and what you may expect in the years ahead. A new "chamber of life" begins when a person has a wake-up call or faces an important question. Such questions are posed by both external (organizational) changes and internal (personal) changes.

The Life Chambers are intended to help you

- Understand how wake-up calls change through your life cycle.
- Identify current and future challenges.

Each chamber contains challenges likely to take place during that life stage. Don't be surprised if your pattern has departed from this general model, that's normal. Genetic, gender, cultural, and historical differences influence one's challenges and timing. Every minute spent on this exercise will make a significant contribution toward taking charge of your life.

15

Life Chambers

In Column A, circle the current challenges most important to you at this point in your life. In Column B, next to each challenge you circled, write in your vision of what you want the outcome to look like.

A. Life Chamber 1   *B. Vision*

Break adolescent ties

Choose lifestyle

Choose work/career direction

Establish financial independence

Handle new work/life relationships

Geographic move; adjust to life on own

Budget costs of living

Life Chamber 2

Settle in work, begin career growth

Select relationships

Achieve autonomy

Become linked to community

Parent

Establish financial options and plans

Handle realities of work changes

A. Life Chamber 3

B. Vision

Clarify personal values

Reappraise relationships

Set long-term goals

Put down roots, achieve
more permanence

Relate to growing children

Reexamine or question initial life
and work commitments

Seek role models or mentors

Life Chamber 4

Manage stress accompanying time demands
(work, family, personal life)

Become involved in broader community

Progress in career and
expand career mastery

Handle increasing financial
obligations

Question values, lifestyle,
and workstyle

Relate to teenage children

Relate to aging parents

A. Life Chamber 5

B. Vision

Adjust to realities of career

Search for purpose

Launch children, adjust to empty nest

Manage mid-life time urgency

Become aware of aging process

Handle increased demands
of older parents

Life Chamber 6

Establish retirement goals

Deepen relationships

Deepen spiritual dimension

Adjust to aging and health changes

Focus on "quality of life"

Do regular financial monitoring

A. Life Chamber 7	B. Vision
Manage stress accompanying retirement choices	
Search for new purpose	
Manage leisure time	
Reevaluate financial plan	
Manage stress of changing relationships and aging process	
Adjust to new housing or life style situations	

Life Chamber 8

Be concerned with personal health care	
Learn to keep learning; open self to new feelings	
Adjust to changing relationships/ letting go	
Search for meaning and legacy	
Explore long-term care options	

The Life Chambers Dialogue

Balancing the tasks and demands of both work and personal life may be the most difficult dilemma confronting you today. The purpose of the Life Chambers Dialogue is to provide a starting point for a discussion of current challenges and future vision. This dialogue results in sharing important thoughts with a partner, who then reciprocates. You serve as catalysts and resources for each other.

First, write in your responses. Then, select a partner. Take turns initiating the discussion. Each of you should complete each sentence stem aloud. Use "I" statements: "I believe ...," "I feel ...," "I am ...." Be as honest with yourself and your partner as you can be.

Life Chambers Dialogue

1. Three key challenges—wake-up calls—in my life that I have learned the most from have been:

_____

_____

_____

2. I discovered from the three key wake-up calls (above) that the way I tend to handle change or transition is to...

_____

_____

_____

3. An important wake-up call coming up for me is...

_____

_____

_____

4. Do I have a clear vision of where I'm going with my work life in the next five years? What is it?

_____

_____

_____

5. Do others (boss, colleagues, mentor) know about my vision? Who knows?

_____

_____

_____

6. Do I have a clear vision for my personal life for the next five years? What is it?

_____

_____

_____

21

7. Do others (family, friends) know about my vision? Who knows?

_____

_____

_____

8. Do I have written work and personal goals?

_____

_____

_____

9. Have I set specific targets and dates for my goals?

_____

_____

_____

Tradeoffs

Many of us say we don't have enough time to take care of our lives and careers. Then, before we know it, we're right!

Too often life just happens. Life evolves without a great deal of thought being directed toward the quality of its days, months, and years, until, as we saw in the last chapter, we get a wake-up call that reminds us of our most precious currency—time.

Many of us have come to acknowledge publicly what we privately knew all along; namely, by successfully surviving adolescence and early adulthood we didn't insure ourselves a tranquil, jolt-free passage through the rest of our life and career. We change, our priorities shift; confidence grows, dissolves into doubt, then back again; relationships evolve; work and lifestyles become static or take on new meanings. Forming a complex web of life patterns, we're either growing or stagnating, building or slipping. Most of us periodically face difficult tradeoffs; a tradeoff means a choice, giving up something to get something else.

Many of us live our lives like the theme in Harry Chapin's song, "Cat's in the Cradle," which deals with a young boy admiring his father and saying that he's "going to be like him." The father is busy and on the run, never really spending the time he promises to the boy.

Life evolves, the son grows and becomes busy. The father ages and becomes less busy. He's more dependent on his contact with his now grown son, but the young adult now takes the dad's position of only promising contact. He has grown up like dad.

This haunting chorus continues throughout the song: "When you comin' home son? I don't know when, but we'll get together then. You know we'll have a good time then."

We all get 168 hours a week to spend. How we make tradeoffs determines the quality of our lives. Do you need a heart attack or cancer or a wake-up call to understand the tradeoffs?

There are times in our work/lives when work is the first priority; and times when relationships take precedence over achievement.

Sören Kierkegaard wrote "Life can only be understood backward, but it must be lived forward." We proceed, at best, with educated guesses about optimal tradeoffs for ourselves.

Tradeoffs always involve the experience of loss. For instance, every time we move in the direction of family or in the direction of work we are cut off from one alternative; we lose it, at least temporarily.

This conflict is our predicament, the dynamic tension that underlies the richness and sadness of our lives.

Think back on your life or look around. How many people really accomplish their important priorities? They stay busy; our society almost mandates that. They make a living. They do some enjoyable things, have leisure activities. But if they knew life were to end soon, how would they feel?

Developing a holistic view of life at work and outside of work and establishing a creative balance between the two is a major challenge today. Throughout the course of life the tradeoffs change. The balancing process depends on learning new ways of managing success by finding satisfactions in one part of life when another part fails to provide satisfactions. Also central to achieving balance is the need to clarify the right personal formula between "living for today" and "living for tomorrow."

Balancing the tradeoffs of both family* and job may be the most difficult and most vexing dilemma confronting many people today. Not only do the problems generated in the workplace spill over into the home; perhaps more significantly, what occurs or does not occur in the family affects performance and stress on the job.

Indeed, the importance of family to individuals cannot be overemphasized. A recent Gallup Poll reports that when asked to name the most important thing in their lives, 84% of those polled answered "my family."

Today's fast-paced social and economic changes are placing greater and greater stresses upon the tradeoff process. How those tradeoffs are resolved will make the difference between a life that enhances a person's ability to be innovative and energized, and one that can easily create a tense, preoccupied, and unproductive person.

The relationship between job performance and family satisfaction is borne out in a stress quotient rating developed by University of Washington psychiatrists Thomas H. Holmes and Richard H. Rahe. The five top causes of stress are, in descending order: the death of a spouse, divorce, marital separation, a jail term, and the death of a close family member.

If a person understands the changes and tradeoffs created as human beings move through various situations in life, the stresses arising from those changes can be managed.

Beyond the normal life tradeoffs that affect us today are the ever-increasing demands that go with the change process and that produce numerous stresses within families. While most organizations profess to value the stable family—they say they want people with happy family lives—today's realities are increasing the stress on the family system with job relocations and demands that the people travel and spend evenings away from home. Globalization and increased overseas travel and transfers from country to country are particularly hard on families.

But perhaps the greatest damage inflicted upon individuals and their families is the image that the media aggressively promotes of the successful corporate executive—self-reliant, certain, and always in control of situations. To conform to this image, many people feel compelled to mask and then deny their normal feelings of inadequacy, dependency, and doubt at work and, too often, in the home as well. The inability to balance and develop the entire range of emotions stifles our ability to understand, participate in, and work through the emotional tradeoffs that every change generates.

Our personal and work lives are interdependent. We're the same person at work and at

---

* "Family" is used here as "any group of people who love and care for each other."

home. We live one life, albeit in different roles and settings. We can set boundaries between these domains, but we can't avoid carrying the baggage of one role into other roles.

Life is a tradeoff for everyone. There is a private belief among many people that somehow they can have it both ways—get what they want without giving up anything that matters to them.

Tradeoffs change with age, health, position, relationships, lifestyles, and reality pressures. The long-term effects of some trade-offs on children, marriage, health, and so on aren't always evident. If tradeoffs are chronically in one direction, the chances of problems developing in the individual and the family are very high.

Success depends in large measure on making effective tradeoffs. Some people measure success internally. Others measure it by wealth, appearance, and position. Some try to find an internal/external balance.

We're used to "keeping score" by comparison. You may define yourself as the sum of what you purchase or produce. But there's always someone wealthier, more attractive, or one rung above you. The prize is always just out of reach.

Try a balanced approach. Put more time into things with no discernible score. Make tradeoffs to include investments in the "internal" quality of each day and in transactions with the significant people in your life. You'll win in the long run, because your life itself will be the prize.

25

The Changes

II

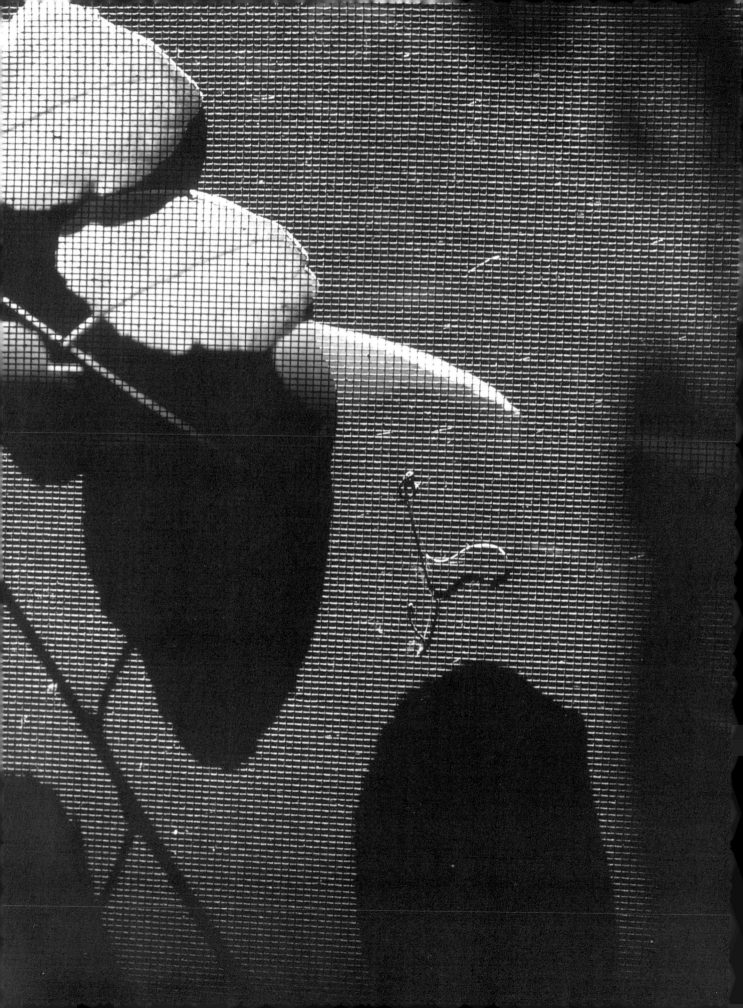

The Growth Curve

"Growth is natural and change is inevitable. But at the key points of change, people often see the new beginning not as an opportunity, but as a threat. To try to stop the growth process, however, is to succumb to Inner Kill— the art of dying without knowing it."

The spiral growth pattern of our chambered nautilus shell is the same as the pattern for human growth. The nautilus represents a way of looking at human growth as a learning process. The nautilus and the Growth Curve (see figures 2-1 to 2-3) show a unifying pattern for growth that is common to a range of living things.

The Growth Curve is based on a model of growth adapted from the ideas of George Land in his book, *Grow or Die*. The Growth Curve may be used as a tool to help an organization or an individual clarify where they are in terms of growth, to help define purpose, or to envision future stages of growth.

Growth is natural and change is inevitable. But at the key points of change, people often see the new beginning not as an opportunity but as a

---

Figure 2-1 The Growth Curve—Phase I. Formative

	Individual	Organization
	Preparing for a Career	Discovering a Pattern
I.	Life/Career Identity	Product/Service Identity
	Vision: "The Dream"	Vision: "Making It"
	Trial and Error	Adapting and Changing
	Task: Self-sufficiency	Task: Survival

---

threat. To try to stop the growth process, however, is to succumb to Inner Kill—the art of dying without knowing it. So why do people resist growth?

To begin, let's examine the larger question of growth from both an organizational and an individual perspective.

The Growth Curve

The model is represented by an "S" curve with three basic phases: Formative, Normative, and Integrative.

I. The Formative Phase

When applied to an organization, the Formative Phase is the stage of the organization's birth, the period in which it searches for an identity and a pattern. This phase is characterized by a strong sense of purpose and vision, a high level of commitment, willingness to take risks, innovation, trial and error, rapid growth, and fun. This phase also includes a good deal of chaos, stress, uncertainty, and yearning for more order and predictability.

In the Formative Phase, the task of the organization is to discover a pattern that works. The key question is "will we survive?"

Working in a Phase I organization is a paradox of excitement and positive energy coupled with tension and insecurity—creative tension fuels rapid growth.

At this stage productive mistakes are acceptable. When you do something that doesn't work, it's a learning opportunity rather than a punishable offense. Compare it to learning to ride a bicycle. Rarely does the ride go smoothly the first time. It requires falling off. Nobody looks at the falls as mistakes. They're simply a necessary part of learning.

The goal of Phase I is to "make it," to succeed, to identify patterns that lead to growth, to become predictable—to get to Phase II.

To put this stage in a personal work/life perspective, think about the beginning of a career. In the beginning stages, we prepare for a career and select an organization or field to get started with. We discover opportunities and develop a work style. We find how we fit the work itself and the organizational culture. We look for a fit—for a place that fits our skills, values, interests, and style. We determine what's required to succeed.

The career learning curve is steep in Phase I. It includes tension and uncertainty about whether we're going to "make it," and a corresponding longing to "test our edges," to grow and to master our chosen job or field. Key words that describe a Phase I career situation are excitement, confusion, learning, hope, frustration, elation, trial and error.

Figure 2-2 The Growth Curve—Phase II. Normative

	Individual (Early)	Organization (Early)
	Building the Career Path	Developing the Pattern
	Life/Career Stability	Systems/Procedures Stability
	Vision: "Success Dream"	Vision: "Doing What You Do Best"
	Learn and Build	Efficient and Effective
	Task: Balancing	Task: Replicating
	(Late)	(Late)
	Extending the Career Path	Extending the Pattern
	Life/Career Drifting	Strategic Drifting
	Vision: "Burnout or Rustout"	Vision: "Grow or Die"
	Master and Improve	Innovating and Maintaining
	Task: Controlling	Task: Strategizing

Late
II. Mid
Early   Back to Basics
I.

Figure 2-2 The Growth Curve—Phase II (continued)

Individual (Back to Basics)	*Organization* (Back to Basics)
Holding on to Job	Holding on to the Pattern
Life/Career Fundamentals	Marketing/Finance Fundamentals
Vision: "Revisit the Dream"	Vision: "Revisit the Good Old Days"
Task: Reworking the Existing Job	Task: Denying the Need to Change

33

II. The Normative Phase

When applied to an organization, the Normative Phase is the stage of steady incremental growth. The pattern for doing business has been discovered and is working.

In the early stage of this phase there is a new stability, more structure and emphasis on efficiency and specialization. The focus is on refinement and development of the pattern. The organization is perfecting its systems and building a management hierarchy. With increased structure often comes less energy and excitement. Roles are decided, and the hierarchy begins to take shape. There are more procedures, guidelines, committees, forms, and levels of decision making.

As the order and stability longed for in Phase I is finally achieved, there is a period of high productivity and profitability because the pattern is being replicated efficiently. Like Phase I, working in a Phase II organization is a mixed experience depending on one's own skills, style, and values.

Mistakes are definitely less tolerated and not viewed as "learning opportunities." They are simply mistakes that need to be engineered out. They shouldn't happen. One way to avoid them is to avoid risk; play it safe. Risk-taking is given lip-service approval: "Yes, we want more innovation...but, be sure not to upset your budget or this quarter's results." Risk-taking is acknowledged but not practiced.

The vision of Phase I is replaced by shorter time frames and outcomes—monthly and quarterly goals. Risk-taking and innovation is relegated to a specific department, like research and development. The task of everyone else is to make the system run efficiently.

The goal of Phase II is to stay there—consistently—enjoying steady incremental growth. The hope is, it will never end.

Think back to the Phase I work/life perspective about beginning a career. Now, in early Phase II, you've established a career path, discovered an identity that is comfortable, and figured out how to fit into the organization's norms and values. You've settled in to a community and a lifestyle, set goals, made plans, and are prepared for a long-term relationship in your field or organization.

Your career in mid-Phase II has begun to bear fruit; you can see what it will take to achieve success. Key words that describe a career at this stage are success, structure, routine, normal, comfortable, profitable, growth, and maintenance.

The timing of this phase depends on your field, industry, organization, and economic environment. Eventually things will begin to change. In late Phase II, the career and job cycle often become routine to the point of boredom. It's predictable, and *that* is trouble. The media is full of stories focusing on the "mid-career crisis" period. There's a natural period of reflection. Life is half over. Who am I? Why am I here? Where am I going? Do I want to continue on this path? What else is there? Do I have enough time? How can I balance my life and work needs and demands?

Late Phase II careers can be described in terms like denial, panic, questioning, burnout, and Inner Kill.

In organizations, late Phase II is characterized by a flattening out of the production cycle. External pressures such as competition, waning product life, increasing costs, and global markets are eroding the pattern.

Internal pressures such as increasing overhead, layers of decision making, and low innovation force the organization to face reality.

Ideally, personally and organizationally, you want to get the curve heading upward again. You genuinely believe you're on the right track, but you've allowed yourself to get fat, dumb, and happy. You've neglected to pay attention to the wake-up calls.

In response to these external and internal pressures, the organization's first move is to go back to basics.

In the hopes of further extending the Phase II pattern that got them there organizations seek to replicate what worked earlier. They cut people, work harder, sell off marginal businesses, reorganize, downsize, and cut costs. There is talk about renewed vision, innovation, marketing, and quality, but the real focus is on extending present practices and procedures. Underlying these actions is an inability to admit that the vision or pattern needs updating.

Back to basics solutions usually work for a while. Innovating, risk-taking, and tightening up the old pattern will get results. But meanwhile the marketplace has shifted. Entrepreneurial competitors have come up with new patterns and solutions.

Figure 2-3 The Growth Curve—Phase III. Integrative

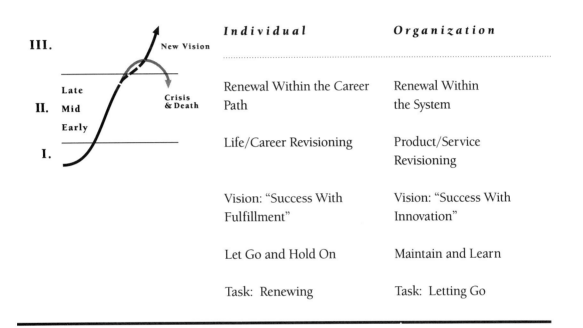

	Individual	Organization
	Renewal Within the Career Path	Renewal Within the System
	Life/Career Revisioning	Product/Service Revisioning
	Vision: "Success With Fulfillment"	Vision: "Success With Innovation"
	Let Go and Hold On	Maintain and Learn
	Task: Renewing	Task: Letting Go

III. The Integrative Phase

When applied to an organization, Phase III is the point at which revisioning occurs and the company looks for a new pattern; once again, an experimenting and learning phase. Often this means renewed or new leadership. Always it means redefining, letting go, innovating, and taking risks. It means walking the line between holding on to the part of the pattern that's working and letting go of the part that's outmoded.

Like Phase I to Phase II, moving to Phase III requires some chaos, uncertainty, and ambiguity. It requires a new leadership thrust—leading the new while managing the old—maintaining the essence of what served the organization well. It requires "intrapreneurs"—champions of new ideas and systems who are willing to take a stand and risk rejection.

Just as the human body will reject a transplanted organ, even though the body's life depends on it, organizations by their nature often work to kill new concepts. Under stress, people will generally opt for control. They will mark time with a wait-and-see attitude. The old ways, although dying, are safer and stronger than the new.

It is imperative, in Phase III, that the organization's leadership set a vision before employees and allow them to define the parts and to put them together. Providing a picture of the future and motivating people to enroll in the vision is the essential task of Phase III leaders. The Phase I learning culture needs to be reinstitutionalized in Phase III.

When applied to personal work/life, Phase III of a career begins a period of uncertainty and the need to plan for new growth and renewal. How rough this period is and whether it is long or short depends not on circumstances and events but on the individual's attitude.

Like corporate cultures, individuals moving into Phase III career situations take apart what they've struggled to create and begin to look at new combinations and new ways of fitting life and work together. They reinvent themselves. Corporate cultures are doing the same.

Career growth usually entails not one change but many. For workaholics, the home life is rediscovered. Many people start beating the bushes looking for balance. They may not know how to define it, but they know they need something besides work to survive.

What Does Phase III Mean to Me?

All organizations and individuals go through phases of growth. It's simply the natural way that things evolve. The Growth Curve helps us understand and anticipate the patterns and phases of growth.

On Figure 2-4 put a check (✔) where you see your career today on the curve. Put an asterisk (*) where you see your organization or workplace today on the curve.

The Growth Curve is general, not specific. It does a better job of describing where an organization or an individual is, and how it got there, than it does at helping you take charge or create the future in any detail.

The *Life Skills* process was designed specifically to meet that need. The first two sections, "The Challenge" and "The Changes," examined the past—how you got to where you are. The next two sections, "Taking Stock" and "Taking Charge," look at a model for creating the future.

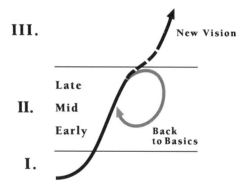

The Life Spiral

The pattern of life, as the Growth Curve illustrates, is to grow. We need to keep reinventing our lives in order to grow. And, the heart of growing is understanding the process: endings–transitions–beginnings.

New beginnings require endings. As the philosopher George Santayana wrote, "Those who cannot remember the past are condemned to repeat it."

Figure 2-5, the Life Spiral, shows the big picture—birth to death. Viewing your life in this way, can put things in a different context. Seeing the interconnected spirals that make up your history and future can assist you in developing a sharper picture of where you have come from...and a clearer vision of where you are headed.

Use the Life Spiral in Figure 2-5 to do the following:

1. Next to the death point, write the age you think you will live to be and the year in which your death will occur.
2. Mark the appropriate midpoint of your life. Write the age you will be (were) at the midpoint. Mark the approximate place you are now. Write your current age next to it. How far along are you in your life? Halfway? Three fourths? One fourth?
3. Many of us experience a definite time in our lives when we move from external expectations to internal considerations—a period of reflection and a move toward taking charge. Draw a line cutting through the model at the place in which you decided to be in charge of your life, to take control and responsibility, and to live your vision. If you have not done this yet, predict when you will.

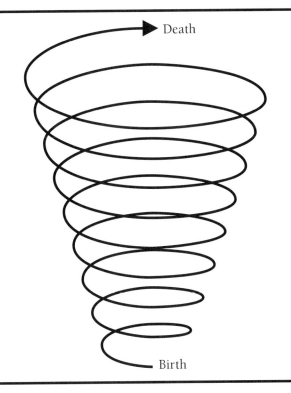

Death

Birth

The Life Spiral

I. Life Plateaus

II. Triggering Events

III. Limbo

· Endings

· Transitions

· Beginnings

IV. Taking Stock

V. Taking Charge

Stages of Change

While navigating the ages and stages of life, you continually let go of and discover new parts of yourself. Letting go is difficult. The only alternative, however, is not to grow, to plateau, to touch life as it passes us by. As Zorba the Greek said, "Life is trouble. Only death is not. To be alive is to undo your belt and look for trouble!"

In achieving growth, you will experience predictable sequences. Change follows this sequence of stages:

Stage I–Life Plateaus

Life seems to be running pretty smoothly. Everything seems in good working order. You may be generally satisfied with your lifestyle, relationship, career, or you can become set in your ways. Most of us can recall being in a situation where we were on a plateau too long. Many of us choose the safe path–comfort zone–and elect to stop growing in order to avoid the work of letting go. We give up. We cover up. We wear masks. We shut down. We experience Inner Kill.

Stage II–Triggering Events

Suddenly things change–voluntarily or involuntarily. You are knocked off balance by a turn of events that reveals new challenges. The most common triggering events are death, divorce, a job change, a health change, spiritual awakening, a physical move, new relationships, deep loss, change in children's lives, retirement, and decade birthdays, (thirty, forty, fifty). These "awakenings" events can act as catalysts. They are wake-up calls.

Stage III–Limbo
(Endings-Transitions-Beginnings)

To insulate yourself from the shock of abrupt change, you may go into a sort of suspended animation or limbo. You withdraw emotionally. Limbo is a feeling of knowing what your life isn't going to be in the future, but not having any notion of what it is going to be. Being in limbo is being immobilized, numb, confused, and not knowing in which direction to turn.

The world's greatest artists, musicians, inventors, scientists, explorers, and leaders have testified repeatedly to the "limbo" dimension of the creative process. The greatest breakthroughs result from a raw moment in which the individual lets go of his or her usual assumptions. To grow is to awaken, to see something different, a possibility. There is an urge to create, to begin anew.

Stage IV–Taking Stock

In this stage you explore solutions— coaching, a new relationship, a book, job renewal, travel, friends, ideas, dreams. You know the answer is out there somewhere; you just have to find it. You explore new ways of behaving. You are excited one day, depressed the next. You are confused, uncertain, exuberant. You seek the solution that will solve your dilemma and make you ultimately happy. Who is the more successful: the person who is unhappy but doesn't make any waves; or the person who searches for expression in life and boldly keeps growing?

Stage V–Taking Charge

Searching has sapped your energy. You seek relief. It's time to take charge, to make a decision so you can stabilize and turn your attention to other elements of life that you have momentarily neglected. A decision is reached. Although perhaps it's not a perfect decision, you start from there.

You recognize that the perfect solution does not exist, that life is a series of changes, each one moving you farther upward in the Life Spiral. As a result, you are more accepting of your experiences. You move ahead with your decisions with more self-confidence and a greater sense of self worth.

Your Five-Year Vision

Viewing your entire life as an ongoing spiral is like seeing a snapshot of the earth taken from outer space. You get a sense of the great but delicate organism that is your existence. But now it's time to zoom in a little and focus on one small part of the spiral.

The Five-Year Vision is a natural, yet expansive, perspective to take. Five years is the amount of time governments often designate for recognizable reform. It's a period after which many farmers plan a crop conversion. It's how long most people take to pay off a car loan! Compared to the Life Spiral, the Five-Year Vision might not seem like much, but compared to how people often operate—just trying to make it to the weekend—it's an eternity.

Envision a Five-Year Vision for your life. It's five years from today. Imagine your ideal day. How are you shaping your space and time so that all your best qualities emerge? What are you doing? Where? To what purpose are you using your talents? Who are your colleagues and clients?

As you develop your vision, be expansive. Aim high. Reach for the stars. Most of us have learned to accept less than our full capabilities—but don't do that here. Find the emotional center of your vision and work from that perspective.

Vision is about creating a mental map. Draw the map of your Five-Year Vision in the space provided. Use words, pictures, diagrams, or whatever you like.

39

My five-year vision looks like this:

The Power of Purpose

In a busy life, the reason for getting up and going to work in the morning often becomes blurred. You need to rediscover your purpose. Everyone needs a clear reason to get up in the morning. We hunger for meaning and purpose in our lives. People want to feel that their lives matter, that they do make a difference. You need to clarify what brings you true satisfaction, the feeling that comes when you can look at your work and priorities and say, "Yes, this is why I get up in the morning."

People without a sense of purpose lack focus in their lives. Focus adds power to actions. Organizations without a sense of purpose also lack focus. In the well-known book, *In Search of Excellence*, one of the authors advises the organization: "Figure out your value system. Decide what your company stands for. Put yourself out twenty years in the future: What would you look back on with the greatest satisfaction?"

The idea of a purpose, for organizations and for individuals, is an idea whose time is now. Great leaders are aware of the power of purpose. Perhaps the most important concept any leader can bring to an organization today is to clarify purpose and to provide a mission statement for leaders and followers alike.

Within the soul of every human being there is a hunger for one's purpose. Everyone wants to know, "Why am I here?" "What is my contribution to life?" Ralph Waldo Emerson gives us a clue: "The purpose of life is not to be happy. It is to be useful, to be honorable, to be compassionate, to have it make some difference that you have lived and lived well."

Purpose is innate. Yet, not everyone has detected or even thought about their purpose.

Others have several purposes. Some people feel they are led to a purpose through spiritual deepening. Others are having a *crisis of purpose*. Some have lost their purpose and are searching for a new one. Many of us fell into ours through someone else, or by a crisis or an unexpected wake-up call.

People today do many things, often with enormous intensity. This pervasive hurry sickness is a sign of the times. It is our fear of wasting or losing time because time is money.

But closer examination may reveal that you're busy hurrying to achieve external recognition for your worth. In reality, much of your life is organized around activities that gain approval; busyness is a way of generating approval.

Finding your way in the world without a sense of meaning and purpose is like hiking in the woods with no map, compass, or sense of direction. Living without a sense of direction or purpose often means striving for results that feel empty or worthless once you have them.

Viktor Frankl, the psychiatrist, author, and Holocaust survivor, has a great viewpoint on the search for meaning. Frankl's work with people in the concentration camps and afterward led him to conclude that when you lose your sense of meaning and purpose in life, psychological and physical ailments are more likely to occur. At the same time, when you rediscover or renew a deeper purpose in life, even the worst crises and most difficult changes can be faced with a sense of power and hope.

In his important book, *Man's Search for Meaning,* he relates how he survived several near-death experiences and how he retained his sense of meaning and purpose. He drew the diagram in Figure 2-6 to illustrate his thinking on meaning.

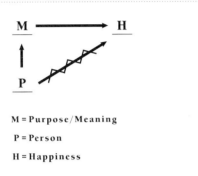

M = Purpose/Meaning

P = Person

H = Happiness

Pursuing a purposeful goal produces happiness, says Frankl, but if we chase happiness directly, we're unlikely to get what we seek. There's no enduring happiness in the symbols of success. Our success in seeking out meaning and purpose for our existence determines the happiness we find.

There are many creative ways to uncover a stronger sense of meaning and purpose for your own life.

Your love for your family, a loved one, your work, your talents, your creative expression, and your commitment to your subordinates all are reasons enough to get up in the morning. You may be waiting to be used for a higher purpose, but the moment hasn't arrived yet. The purpose of the *Life Skills* process is to help individuals reflect on and express their unique purpose in life.

Most of us know that the secret of enduring happiness isn't found in external success only. Yet we persist in aspiring to the version of fulfillment set out by the media and then regard ourselves as inadequate for failing to achieve it.

Why is it that every society seems to honor its live conformists and its dead mavericks? Why are people like Socrates, Gandhi, Churchill, and Jesus scorned in their own times for their purposefulness and honored after their deaths when it was safe to do so? The easy way out is to be normal; hide your vision, if you have one, and be like everyone else. There will always be plenty of critics. As Albert Einstein said, "Great spirits have always encountered violent opposition from mediocre minds."

Of course, the case for purpose has never rested on provable facts or rational logic. Purpose relies on intuition and on the release of human energies generated by hope. *The capacity for hope is the most significant fact in life.*

Purpose Is Necessary for Inspired Performance

One of the best kept secrets in organizations today is that people want to "make a difference." People in many organizations feel that they don't make a difference. They see themselves as victims of external forces beyond their control.

A clear alignment between organizational and personal purpose can create organizations capable of inspired performance. Power is created when people see their organization's purpose as an extension of their personal purpose.

They're able to identify with the organization and consciously assume responsibility for its success. Purpose is exemplified in that profound level of teamwork that characterizes exceptional sports teams and symphony orchestras. Many of us are jaded by our past experiences in purposeless organizations. We can't even imagine what one might be like. Yet most of us have experienced being part of a project team, community or religious group, or sports or music unit that brought out our best.

Placing importance on purpose clarifies basic direction. Clearly, an organization's purpose is the basis for sound strategic planning. Perhaps more important, organizational purpose provides the opportunity for shared meaning among employees. A clear alignment of personal and organizational purpose can provide a deeper reason of what we "want to stand for."

Purpose embodies our highest values and aspirations. It inspires us to reach for what could be. It lifts us beyond petty day-to-day barriers. Purpose enables us to clarify and realize what we really want, independent of what seems possible. It often encourages us to keep our agreements and commitments with others in our organization because of our deeply felt personal commitment and common bond.

The *Life Skills* process assumes that people want to

- Contribute to the organization; to make a difference.
- Express unique talents and to make unique contributions.
- Understand the purpose of their organization and the vision of their leaders.
- Have a strong hand in determining what to do and how to do it.
- Be accountable for results and want to be both recognized *and* rewarded for their achievements.

Although not new, the quest for aligning personal and organizational purpose is a noteworthy development of our time. It touches people of all ages and all walks of life. It reflects a profound dissatisfaction and disenchantment with overly materialistic values and the greed that often accompanies them. People are seeking a vision that will lift them above a perspective that has proven itself incapable of offering fulfillment.

Organizations, like individuals, need a reason for being. Peter Drucker argues convincingly that the key question every company must put to itself periodically is "What business are we in?" Every leader and manager is eventually haunted by this same question.

Certainly the ultimate goal of any business is to survive and grow. But to increase productivity a business needs another reason for being; it needs to serve people and society in a very special way, to make a real difference in the lives of all who are influenced by it.

A sense of purpose accompanies inspired performance. Those who take the idea of purpose most seriously are the leaders and managers in this country's most successful companies. Many once-successful companies have gone under because they became so involved in markets, competition, and pricing that they lost sight of their purpose. They forgot to keep asking, "What business are we in?" "How are our customers' and employees' lives upgraded because of our product or service?" A company that provides products and services without a purposeful desire to serve has a very good chance of failing.

Working *on purpose* is simply a superior way to do business. It means clearly and honestly deciding and communicating what business the company is in and focusing collective energies accordingly. The questions we ask in determining organizational purpose are the very same ones that effective and purposeful individuals ask:

- Who are we?
- Why are we here?
- What are our talents?
- What do we have to contribute that is unique or different?
- What special technology or knowledge do we have?
- What do we value?
- What needs are we uniquely qualified to meet?

The result is a statement of the mission of the organization, along with the values and commitments that drive it. Organizations with leaders, managers, and employees who regularly ask such questions discover that new products, services, and ways of doing business often evolve and that the core personal values people wish to have in their work are satisfied.

Thomas Peters and Robert Waterman in their book, *In Search of Excellence,* found that top executives of excellent companies ensure that no corporate decision affecting internal or external practices goes against the company's purpose. They realize that it takes only a few lapses in company purpose for internal integrity to be lost.

Excellent companies understand the value of purpose and emphasize its importance in company policies and practices. *In Search of Excellence* confirms that a purpose-driven business organization is not only conceivable but also desirable in financial and human terms. Leaders of excellent companies under-

stand that they really can't compel people to do anything. They can only encourage them to *want* to do things. They understand that real commitment does not come through autocratic power, but through the "power of purpose."

Purpose is something you do every day. It's not something in an annual report or on a plaque in the reception area. It's to be acted out. Customers aren't fooled. They compare what organizations say their mission and values are with what they do; they compare what they say with what their behavior is. In an organization with integrity, customers and employees know that the visions, statements, and promises they hear are accurate.

Organizational purpose is more difficult to evaluate than individual purpose. We can compare the statements of our friends with their actions. In an organization, however, we need to evaluate the collective intent of the leadership. We need to compare their words with their actions.

Purpose Is Necessary for Health

Why do so many people die within twenty-four months or so of retiring? Having a purpose for living obviously stimulates the will to live. There's a reason to get up in the morning; one's life takes on a larger significance.

Many people who have overcome serious disease were able to identify some important life purpose or goals early in their healing process. After studying the case histories of people who overcame serious diseases, Norman Cousins noted that all of them had experienced some type of crisis just before their illness was diagnosed. Studies have

43

shown that the most common emotional state preceding the diagnosis of cancer is a sense of hopelessness and despair.

There's much wisdom in the words of Nietzsche: "He who has a why to live for can bear almost any how." What people need for optimum wellness is the striving for some goal or purpose that moves them.

If experience alone brought wisdom and joy, then all older adults would be happy, enlightened masters. But, wisdom and joy don't come automatically with age. Purpose can't be ordered into being. It must be discovered. We need to encourage people to rediscover themselves at various ages. They need to be given support for the naturalness of this quest.

With purpose we gain clarity, direction, and relatedness to the greater whole. Purpose provides a reason to live.

Purpose Provides Focus

There's no general agreement on what the purpose of life is, but those who are healthiest in body and soul seem to have defined for themselves a purpose for living. Not only does it serve as a reason for living, but it becomes a lodestar—the point at which one focuses one's day-to-day energies.

George Bernard Shaw captured this truth:

> This is the true joy in life the being used for a purpose recognized by yourself as a mighty one; one being thoroughly worn out before you are thrown on the scrap heap; the being a force of Nature instead of a feverish selfish little clod of ailments and grievances complaining that the world will not devote itself to making you happy...

Taking Stock

III

The Taking Stock Inventory

47

"Life is not a

dress rehearsal."

Too often life just happens. Life evolves without a great deal of thought directed toward the quality of its days, months, and years.

To be sure, every day each of us has a myriad of feelings racing through our mind and body: joy, frustration, fear, sadness, anticipation, and so on. Perhaps it's time to recognize a fact.

Life is not a dress rehearsal.

Rather than getting so caught up in events and happenings, it's critical to devote some serious reflection to what is happening. In essence, the Taking Stock Inventory is a quality-of-life balance sheet. Just as in finance, the objective is to end up with assets exceeding liabilities, the result being net worth.

Just as it makes sense to periodically review your financial and physical health, it's important to assess your personal well being on a regular basis. An easy way of getting in touch with many of life's issues is to thoughtfully take stock.

The Concept of Taking Stock

The Taking Stock Inventory is based on observations and studies into the lives and careers of individuals noted for leading balanced, successful lives. Ten dimensions characterize the quality of life of these people.

You may wonder why it's important to inventory your quality of life. When you confront change, it's important to make choices in a manner consistent with what you really value.

The Taking Stock Inventory is a self-assessment process designed to help you evaluate how effectively you manage your career and life interests and pursuits. It is designed to help you measure your quality of life and to think through your growth options. The questions in the Inventory offer a systematic method, based on your past and present experiences, of explaining how you perceive yourself.

The Taking Stock Inventory gives you a snapshot of your "self-image," your wants, and your values. It also provides reasons for choices, because you're likely to try to fulfill your own self-image. Most of us try to make sense out of our lives and careers and, therefore, attempt to build a coherent and acceptable self-image.

How to Do the Inventory

Plan to spend at least two hours on the activities in this section. You don't have to complete them without interruption, but you do need to select a partner for Step 2. We recommend the following procedure:

Step 1: (One Hour)
Answer the Inventory questions in your own words. Write in your responses.

Step 2: (One Hour)
Select a partner with whom you can be reasonably open and frank about quality-of-life issues. A spouse or close friend can be a good partner. In an organization it's best to avoid a superior or subordinate; peers can work well if they feel comfortable with one another. Interviewing across organizational levels can be unproductive

because a person may hide information in order to impress a person who's at a different level in the organization.

The dialogue should take a minimum of sixty minutes.

Your partner takes notes in your book while you talk without distraction.

What's important in this process is caring, not curing. Listening and asking the right questions are critical. Your dialogue partner should lead you to greater self-insight so that you can take charge of your own choices.

Step 3:

Read the "Ten Dimensions of Quality of Life," which follows the Taking Stock Inventory.

49

Taking Stock Inventory

1. Time

How would you describe your typical daily schedule? Do you have time for your real priorities? What's your most important time need at this point in your life?

My Insights: **My Partner's Insights:**

2. Values

What are your top three values at this point in your life? Have you had a pattern of taking the necessary risks to live your values ("walk your talk")? What's one values-driven risk you've taken recently?

My Insights: **My Partner's Insights:**

3. Vitality

How do you spend your leisure time? Are you having fun? What do you currently do for fun?

My Insights: **My Partner's Insights:**

4. *Purpose*

How would you answer the question, "Why do I get up in the morning?" Do you have a clear sense of purpose? Can you describe it or write it down?

My Insights: **My Partner's Insights:**

5. *Career*

Did you choose your career or did it choose you? How did you arrive at this phase of your career? Think of several times in your career when you really loved what you were doing. Discuss these "peak moments" to see what they tell you about the conditions and goals that motivate you.

My Insights: **My Partner's Insights:**

6. *Spirituality*

How would you describe your spiritual life at this point in your life? Do you set aside time for quiet and contemplation? What principles govern your personal actions?

My Insights: **My Partner's Insights:**

7. Health

How would you describe your health? Are you comfortable with your physical self? Do you exercise? Do you relax? Do you drink? Smoke? Do you have as much energy as you'd like?

My Insights: **My Partner's Insights:**

8. Talents

What natural talents do people recognize in you? What are your most enjoyed talents?

My Insights: **My Partner's Insights:**

9. Relationships

Do you talk about what's important to you? Who do you talk to? Do you have friends? Are you lonely or rich in relationships?

My Insights: **My Partner's Insights:**

10. Money

How much annual income do you need to support your current lifestyle? How is your financial health? Do you have written financial goals and plans?

My Insights: **My Partner's Insights:**

Summary

Using a scale of 1 to 10 (10 being very satisfied), how satisfied are you with each factor of your quality of life?

Time	_____	**Purpose**	_____	**Health**	_____	**Money**	_____
Values	_____	**Career**	_____	**Talents**	_____		
Vitality	_____	**Spirituality**	_____	**Relationships**	_____		

What two areas would you most like to improve?

The next ten sections provide insights and exercises to work on the areas where you'd like to improve. Complete the two that reflect your highest-priority growth motivators.

Ten Dimensions of Quality of Life

The ten dimensions represent ten attitude and activity orientations that seem to be consistently evident in balanced, successful individuals. "Success" is used here in the broadest sense, referring to success in personal as well as work life. The goal for each person is to develop and maintain a satisfying balance among the ten dimensions.

The Taking Stock Inventory helps identify strengths along with areas for further growth and development in these dimensions:

1. Time

Successful people spend their time currency effectively. We all struggle with time conflicts that require trade-offs. The price of improving one quality of life area usually means spending less time in another.

Some of the other areas must necessarily become less important. Time resourcefulness is a matter of a) deciding where to let go, and b) accomplishing more in less time so that more time is available for other activities.

Further Reading: *The Organized Executive* by Stephanie Winston

2. Values

Successful people have clear values. They seem to be efficient judges of situations, carefully thinking through the risks and outcomes of each to determine if it could be lived with. They're usually not willing to do things they wouldn't like to have public.

Further Reading: *Man's Search for Meaning* by Viktor Frankl

3. Vitality

Successful people are satisfied with their health, energy, and vitality. Vitality means to have animation, vigor, and liveliness; the opposite of Inner Kill. Many people believe that a vital person devotes time and energy to each quality of life dimension. Achieving vitality depends on an individual's point of view, values, and goals.

Further Reading: *When All You've Ever Wanted Isn't Enough* by Harold Kushner

4. Purpose

Successful people understand the difference between goals and purpose. They have a reasonable idea of where the world is headed and their place and purpose in it. Visions, goals, and risks are all based on a clear sense of purpose and direction. They're confident that their role is important and that they can make a difference in their world.

Further Reading: *The Power of Purpose* by Richard J. Leider

5. Career

Successful people have a career dream worth dreaming. They often use their top talents on something they believe needs doing in their world or their organization. They're not just putting in their time, waiting for the weekend or early retirement. They enjoy stretching and view work not just as a means to an end. They probably set financial career goals, but do so mostly for the convenience of keeping score.

Further Reading: *The Inventurers* by Janet Hagberg & Richard J. Leider

6. Spirituality

Successful individuals have a basis of faith in a higher power. They also have a basic faith in themselves and take personal responsibility for living their faith. They believe in the ultimate triumph of good and have a faith in and respect for others as well. They're conscious of their connection to nature and the environment. They sense the universal bond that connects us all.

Further Reading: *The Road Less Traveled* by M. Scott Peck

7. Health

Successful people take care of their physical well-being. They manage stress well.

They're seldom workaholics. They juggle many interests and demands at work and at play. They don't allow their physical conditioning to chronically take a back seat to work demands.

Further Reading: *Wellness Workbook* by Regina Ryan and John Travis

8. Talents

Successful individuals understand and use their special talents and skills. They spend time acquiring knowledge and developing their talents for personal and professional development. They understand that people usually succeed at things they enjoy doing. This doesn't mean avoiding unpleasant tasks; it does mean making changes to align their work with their most enjoyed talents.

Further Reading: *7 Kinds of Smart* by Thomas Armstrong

9. Relationships

Successful people take steps to create effective networks of productive relationships. They have intimate people in their lives whom they are willing to turn to in times of need. One of the values of true friendship is the ability to listen to each other. When the need arises they have a friend who is there.

They're also willing to return the favor. They let their feelings out in a constructive fashion. They don't mask their feelings. They enjoy a full range of emotions from love to anger to admiration to jealousy to pain to joy. Often they have mentors or support groups to learn from.

Further Reading: *Transitions* by William Bridges

10. Money

Successful individuals know that financial well-being is far more likely when one sets specific and high goals. Yet, they know the difference between challenge and fantasy. They divide goals into manageable chunks, and monitor their progress to get feedback and get more enjoyment out of life. They realize that joy comes not just because of the financial rewards of success but because of the journey. Life itself is the reward.

Further Reading: *Voluntary Simplicity* by Duane Elgin

Time

Time management is becoming the subject of more and more books and seminars. A complex and fast-changing society seems to lend itself to a myriad of time pressures. We're constantly interrupted, overburdened, dealing with a crisis, or striving to meet deadlines. The inevitable result is any one of the following symptoms:

- Constant busyness
- Buildups of stress
- Not enough hours in the day
- Unfinished work
- Unfulfilled personal goals
- Relationship superficiality
- Lack of fun

What's going on? Why do we get in these binds? Why are we less productive than we should be? Why do we only scratch the surface of our potential?

Alec MacKenzie, the renowned time management specialist, says that all individuals in all countries have similar ways to waste time. Among them are

- Lack of objectives, priorities, or planning
- Attempting too much at once
- Interruptions
- Crisis management
- Ineffective delegation
- Meetings
- Procrastination
- Personal disorganization
- Inability to say "no"

Two simple concepts can help you counter the insidious time wasters noted above.

1. Be clear about your priorities.
2. Say "no" often.

Since it isn't the purpose of this book to focus solely on the issue of time management, we'll share what we consider to be some excellent sources devoted exclusively to that subject. Each of these books contains basic points that are consistent with the central theme of this work.

Getting Organized by Stephanie Winston

How to Get Control of Your Time and Your Life by Alan Lakein

The Organized Executive by Stephanie Winston.

The Time Trap by Alec MacKenzie

For other ideas about time management see Section VI, "Not Enough Hours in the Day."

Life Rhythms

In our culture, busyness is a status symbol. Many of us oversubscribe our time and then wonder why we feel overwhelmed or have no time to finish anything. Even our leisure time is heavily scheduled. As a result, sometimes we experience an "energy crisis."

Have you ever imagined how different your days would be if you did things at your own pace, if you chose how to expend your energies during the 168 hours you had available each week?

Of course, you have responsibilities that can't just be abandoned. But you certainly can consider your lifestyle in terms of your time and energy.

What is your present attitude toward time? Does it rule you or have you mastered it? Are you killing time or creating it? If you did find your own sense of time by which to live, in what ways would you change your life?

A Life Rhythm is your own individual sense of timing, the natural pace at which you're most comfortable living your own life.

Daily Life Rhythm

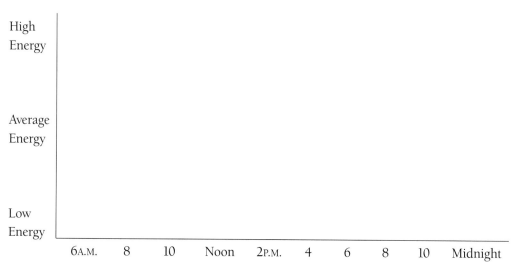

Directions:

a. Map your daily life rhythm by pinpointing the times of day that your energy level is high or low. Draw a moving line to connect the points.

b. Mark the high and low point of the day.

c. How does your cycle relate to your schedule? Do you do your most creative or taxing work at the high or low energy points in your day? Do you work best in long or short cycles?

d. Does your spouse or closest friend live by similar rhythms? If not, how do you adapt to each other?

e. Is your rhythm a result of what is expected of you or of your own needs?

The Time Journal

One useful way to learn about your time priorities is to recall what you actually do on a daily basis. What type of activities do you engage in? How do you allocate your time among job, family, entertainment, sleep, and other activities? Who do you interact with, in what way, and how often?

Even in work settings that are highly structured, or on the most typical days, the way in which you approach time says something about you. Regardless of the setting, we're always faced with choices. Patterns in those choices, like life rhythms, can tell us something about ourselves.

Our impressions of what we normally do are often vague and inaccurate. A reliable method is to keep a log or journal of your activities throughout one full day.

Pause every hour and make a few notes regarding what you've been doing. (Your comments don't have to be lengthy.) Most people can remember in some detail what they have been doing for the past hour or two. Examine your time journal for evidence to support themes from the Taking Stock Inventory.

For example, some journals are very methodical with entries recorded at regular intervals. Some journals are full of names and human interactions. Some are recorded in short, terse phrases; others read like a novel. Some describe a fast-moving, active person; others a slow-moving, reflective person. Some describe people who jump from one activity to another, while others describe people who concentrate on one task until it is completed.

By identifying patterns in a journal and drawing careful insights from those patterns, you can reinforce or contradict themes that have emerged in your Taking Stock Inventory.

Time Journal

Values

It has become popular for people to talk about their values. Probably fewer than ten people out of one hundred, however, have really examined their lives and the values that drive day-to-day behavior.

A value is a thing or condition that you consistently act on to get or to keep. Thus, the more consistently and energetically you commit your time or money to something, the more you apparently value it. This means that you can get a pretty clear idea of your values by studying your calendar and your checkbook.

Living your values means living "awake." The ability to clarify your values and to commit energies toward them means having a definite approach to a defined quality of life.

How many people do you know who drift with their life circumstances, accepting less than life has to offer and taking no risks to create a definite approach to life? How long has it been since you asked yourself, "What do I want out of life?" "How am I spending my precious time currency?" "What are my values?"

But from where do values emerge? How can you clarify them in your life? For many of us, reflection is as tough as it is inevitable. For every person who summons up the courage to explore their values, there are many who hurry on hoping that busyness will feed their hunger while they wait for some special event or person to point the way.

Every year, hundreds of high school and college commencement speakers exhort new graduates to "make a difference, to make commitments, to believe in something, to matter!"

How would you respond? You've accepted an invitation to make a short commencement address at your alma mater (high school or college). What do you say to today's youth? They've asked you to tell them your values, philosophy of life, your keys to a successful life. The only thing they have in common is that every one of them wants to succeed in his or her own unique way.

First, use the questions that follow as a warm-up to writing your commencement address.

Life Values

John Donne said, "No man is an island." Martin Luther King spoke of the "web of mutuality." Other people often have great influence on our lives.

Identify three people who've had the deepest impact on your life (at least one outside your family). What specific advice, philosophy, or value has stuck with you?

Name _____ Value _____

Name _____ Value _____

Name _____ Value _____

List three books, tapes, movies, poems, sermons, or sayings that have contributed to your own values. What insight has stuck with you?

Resource _____ Insight _____

Resource _____ Insight _____

Resource _____ Insight _____

Tennyson in *Ulysses* says, "I am part of all I have met." List five peak experiences that have profoundly shaped your life/career direction.

Experience _____ Value _____

Experience _____ Value _____

Experience _____ Value _____

Experience _____ Value _____

Experience _____ Value _____

Commencement Address

Use the following space to record the highlights of a five-minute speech to today's graduates at your high school or college. Share what you've learned, what you know is right, and what you know will work because you've experienced it. Summarize the key points.

63

What values matter most in your life at this moment? Obviously, each person's interests and needs are focused on different activities at various life stages. Think back to major values you've held in the past. How different are your values today?

All of us live in a dynamic environment. Job requirements, people, and economics will be different tomorrow than they are today. We're often reminded that it's no longer possible to settle into a predictable pattern for a lifetime.

To explore your values is to become more thoroughly aware of your priorities and, consequently, to live in closer harmony with your beliefs. Value clarification helps develop the ability to make decisions about the direction of your life and work. By discovering your values, you can shape what you want.

In the process of clarifying your values, a gap might arise between what you say your values are and how you actually behave. The following five criteria can be used to determine whether you actually hold a value or not.

Choosing a Value

1. Did you choose it freely? (not forced upon you by others)
2. Did you choose from alternatives? (consider your options)
3. Did you give it thoughtful consideration?
4. Are you willing to commit to the choice publicly?
5. Do you carry out the choice day to day?

Full Value: Fulfills all five criteria above.

Partial Value: Fulfills some but not all five criteria above.

Work Values

A key step in clarifying your priorities is to be clear about the answer to the question, "Why do I work?"

Values play a critical role in career satisfaction. Look honestly at what you need and want.

During times of change, the need to understand your work values is more important than at other times. You might find, for example, you have grown out of familiar roles; certain images of yourself no longer fit. Organizational changes have a way of forcing values decisions, and choices are easier when your values are clear.

Values help you to make sense of the world. Every decision you make is based on (1) your values, and (2) the facts of the situation. The facts you listen to are often selected on the basis of personal values.

Work values are formed by experiences with other people, family members, teachers, and groups to which you belong. All of these have a powerful effect on the shaping and formation of values.

Values are not right or wrong or true or false. They are personal preferences. Exploring your preferences may be somewhat difficult.

65

Work Values

Step 1
Figure 3-1 charts a number of desirable Work Values for your ideal job. Select the ten most important to you now (whether or not you currently have them).

Step 2
Rank your ten values from "most important" (1) to "least important" (10) according to your values now.

Step 3
List below your five most important values from 1 (most important to you) to 5.

1. _____

2. _____

3. _____

4. _____

5. _____

From your most important values (step 3), list those provided by your current job and those you need more of to be fully satisfied. Write them in the spaces provided.

Of my five "most important" values, my job satisfies these:

_____

_____

_____

_____

_____

Of my top values, in my current job I need more of these:

_____

_____

_____

_____

_____

Knowing what you want from your work also means knowing how important each value is to you. All of the work values you have selected are important. In most career situations, however, you have to make hard choices among them. Sometimes you give up certain values in order to get others.

Figure 3-1 Work Values Matrix

Security
A job that is not likely
to be eliminated: assurance
of career longevity and a
reasonable financial reward.

Recognition
Self and work known and
approved by others; job
viewed as important in the
organization; well regarded
in one's field; public
credit for work well done;
recognized expert.

Comfort
Low pressure; few constraints;
job that is largely predictable;
opportunity to let others set
expectations and direction;
contentedness; enjoyable,
leisurely life; avoid "rat race"
in job role.

Advancement
A job that provides
opportunity to grow, move
up the ladder; possibly to get
ahead rapidly; aspiring; title.

Environment
Pleasant working
conditions; workplace
that is clean and well
designed.

Relationships
Belonging; working with
a team; frequent and open
interpersonal contact with
others; develop close personal
relationships as a result of work
activity; friendly, compatible
environment.

Contribution
Opportunity to have a
direct impact on the success
of the organization; making
a lasting contribution or
legacy.

Variety
New and different challenges;
opportunity for much new
learning; frequent changes
in content and setting.

Adventure
Situations with excitement and
flair; job that demands best use
of your resources and abilities
to meet new situations. Frequent
risk-taking with possible loss or
gain involved.

67

Figure 3-1 Work Values Matrix (continued)

Independence
Make decisions about one's work; manage oneself; opportunity to work independently according to my time schedule; self-reliant, do project by myself.

Entrepreneurship
Motivation to be self-employed; to develop a new product or service; desire to define oneself through one's work; profit/gain through ownership.

Creativity
Solving new problems and tasks well according to one's own standards; opportunity to innovate and create new ideas, programs, products, etc.; chance to create and finish something important.

Purpose
A job that helps people; improving society; service resulting in benefits to others; moral value; feel that my work is contributing to ideals I feel are very important.

Challenge
Chance to tackle something important; problem-solving as core part of job; work in time-pressured circumstances; role that pits my abilities against others; high pace activity; competition.

Leadership
Responsibility for directing the work of others; to be held accountable for important tasks; authority and power to decide courses of action, policies, etc; influence people.

Money
Purchase essentials and luxuries; prosperous lifestyle; gain respect of friends, family, community. High earnings anticipated.

Balance
Job that leaves time for pursuits outside of work; duties that leave time for community, family, and vocational pursuits.

Location
Geographic location conducive to lifestyle; community where I can become involved; relocation options.

Vitality

Your willingness to live your values, is what vitality is all about. Vitality has two dimensions, outer and inner. An integrated life expresses a blend of reflection and expression. (see Figure 3-2)

Figure 3-2
Dimensions of Vitality

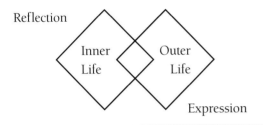

There's often a wide gulf between what we think (reflection) and what we do (expression). To have vitality requires steady work. At different times in our life, we take stock. We recharge our batteries. We question our intentions.

By activating our vitality through the Life Skills process we create the quality of our life. This is a task that requires daily attention and practice. We become vital persons only by making daily commitments.

In every situation, we have the freedom and the possibility of deciding for or against the influence of our surroundings. Although we may seldom choose, it's always open to us to do so.

Viktor Frankl, in a moving description of inmates of the concentration camps during World War II, describes men and women who, under the most adverse circumstances, were able to "do differently"...to choose to care for others, in a situation in which every external human freedom was denied.

From them we learn, says Frankl, that freedom is not something we "have" and therefore can lose, it is what we "are." It's our deepest potential, only needing to be called upon.

Human freedom is "freedom to," and it's our central task to use our freedom to create the quality and vitality of our lives.

The process in *Life Skills* is not new. The essential questions have been asked for thousands of years. Yet, we must ask and answer these questions for ourselves in our own way.

When we fail to explore and get excited over the possibilities that are open to us, we stop growing and join the ranks of Inner Kill, those who are tiptoeing through life in order to make it safely to death.

Viktor Frankl addressed the vitality issue in *Unheard Cry for Meaning* in this way:

> For too long we have been dreaming a dream from which we are now waking up: the dream that if we just improve the socioeconomic situation of people, everything will be okay, people will become happy. The truth is that as the struggle for survival has subsided, the question has emerged: survival for what? Evermore people today have the means to live, but not meaning to live for.

Frankl claims that even in very successful lives there are a high percentage complaining of a deep sense of futility. He suggests that mid-life crisis may truly be a crisis of meaning and vitality. Taking a new look at your life at this stage may be in order.

Mid-Life Vitality

Take a few minutes to jot your reflections on these questions.

1. As a child, people seemed "old" when they began to

2. Seeing my parents grow older (or die) has caused me to

3. The thing that causes me to feel most vital at this point in my life is

4. Imagine that you can travel anywhere in the world for a weekend to consult with any older heroes or models from whom you'd like some advice. Who would you choose as your advisor? On what kinds of challenges or questions would you ask advice?

Advisor   *Key Questions You'd Ask*

_____   _____

_____   _____

_____   _____

_____   _____

What do your questions tell you about yourself? Your future? Your vitality?

Vitality is a complex issue. It's not a mechanical formula with five points on how to live a better life. It is an issue reserved for people who are willing to look inside themselves, it's for the spouses and significant others who want to understand and support what their partner really thinks and feels.

Vitality is a deep issue. It's an issue for people who have the courage to embrace the opportunities life presents. It's an issue for the individual who doesn't want to sit at his or her retirement dinner, inwardly wondering, "was it really worth it?"

At times during your life, vitality wanes, and you ask, "How can I escape this sleep?"

In some cases, you can't wake up without help. You need to rely on people who aren't asleep or who don't fall asleep so easily. List those people who have the ability to give you that periodic wake-up call to the possibilities of your life and work.

Two people who wake me up or keep me vital:

1. _____

2. _____

Vitality and Play

Exploring your feelings about enjoyment of life is an essential step toward improving and maintaining vitality. Play is a primary life activity. There's nothing more characteristic about children than their love of play. But, play can be more difficult than work for adults!

What happens to play as we grow older? As adults, we often look at play as serving some "utilitarian" purpose like losing weight, reducing stress, or training for a sport. For many of us physical education classes turned play into boredom, pleasure into work.

There are many ways to enjoy yourself, often at little cost. There's no reason why you shouldn't have fun in the process of living. Play influences the rest of what you do and how you do it.

Routine living and too many amenities may dull one's emotions. Away from routine and in a play situation, emotions surge up and are released to reveal part of the meaning of what it is to be fully vital.

Why do people leave the comfort and security of their daily routines for adventures like mountaineering, rafting, scuba diving, running a marathon, and other activities that subject them to stress and risk? Specific rewards of adventure vary with the activity. Obviously, people engage in these activities for their unique natural values, qualities that they don't experience in their daily routines.

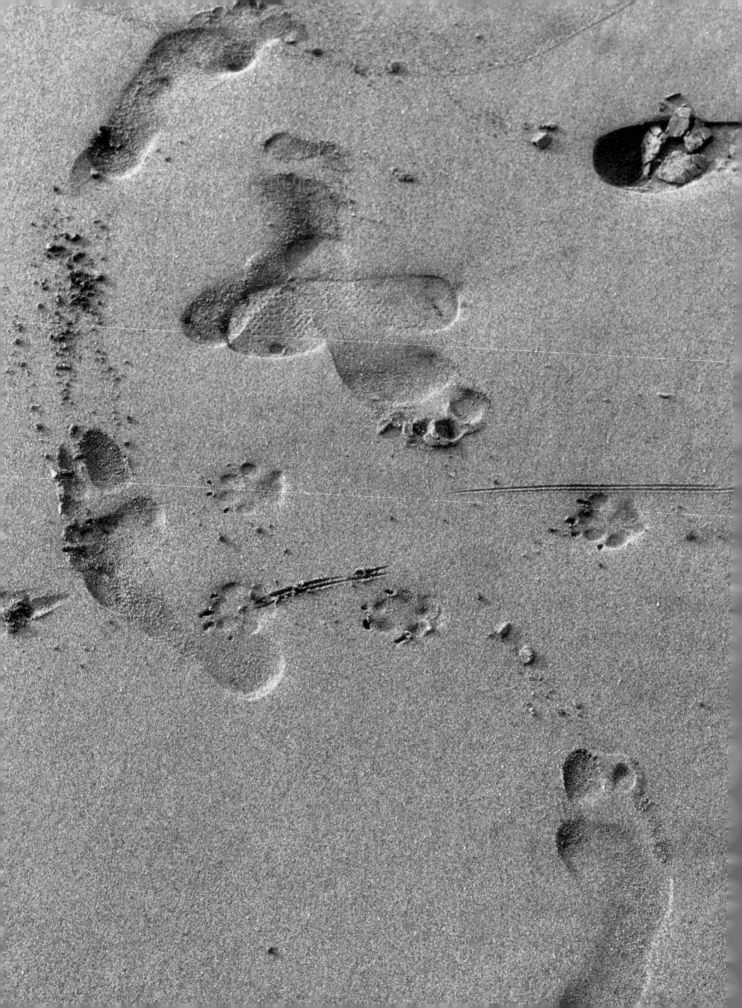

Purpose

It all starts with purpose. Who am I? Why am I here? What am I striving for? What's the point of working? What difference does my life make?

By purpose, we mean your intention, something toward which you are always striving. A goal is not a purpose. A goal is concrete, with a start and a finish. A purpose keeps going. It gives meaning and direction to our lives. Purpose is the road; goals are stops along the road.

Other people often try to tell you what your purpose should be. From the time you are born, people try to distract you from your inner purpose and assign you their own values.

The world is incomplete until each one of us names and expresses our purpose for living and working. The search for purpose is a search for some reassurance of our uniqueness. Each of us wants to leave our own unique "footprints."

What will your "footprints" be like? What would you like to see etched on your tombstone or preached from a pulpit at your funeral? A goal in life can be to "be successful," to make money, but would you feel comfortable with that as your purpose in life? Would you like the epitaph on your tombstone to be your average salary for the last three years? Envision now your epitaph. What do you really want it to say? Write it in the space provided.

Living in accordance with your purpose is called "integrity"—behaving in a way that makes you feel good about yourself, day in and day out. One of the best ways to help you stick to your purpose, to live your epitaph, is to use the Two-Year Test.

I would like my epitaph to say:

Two-Year Test

If your life were to end in two years, would it be complete? What would be left undone? What would be unsaid? How would you spend your precious time during those two years? Could you look at yourself in the mirror at the end of those two years without guilt? When you live on purpose, you can look yourself straight in the eye.

The case for purpose has never rested on provable facts or rational assessment. Purpose by nature is independent of logic. What gives purpose its power is the release of human energies generated by the longing for something better. The capacity for purpose is the most significant fact in life. It gives human beings a sense of destination and the energy to get started.

Purpose can't be ordered into practice. People in a condition of transition can't be commanded to follow a leader's noble vision.

But they can be encouraged to rediscover themselves. They can be given confidence in the naturalness of their own vision. Thinking, feeling, complaining, creating—the purposeful individual has become more important to organizations than ever before.

The most fortunate people on earth are those who have found an idea that is bigger than they are, a vision that moves them and fills their lives with interest, energy, and challenge. As Victor Hugo put it: "Nothing in this world is so powerful as an idea whose time has come." There's never been a shortage of good ideas; but there has always been a shortage of purposeful people who will risk taking a stand with their lives or their work.

In a sentence or two, try to write clearly your life purpose in the following exercise. Be honest with yourself. You can't fool life, and you don't want to fool yourself.

My purpose in life is...

If you find it difficult to write down your purpose in life, don't be discouraged. Live in the question for a few days or weeks. The effort will have lasting benefits.

Many factors go into purpose, but on one factor, most people who study personal effectiveness agree: The deepest satisfaction comes from making a difference in the lives of others.

> For the best mental health, for the greatest emotional maturity, the individual should have a cause, a mission, an aim in life that is constructive and that is so big he has to keep working on it.
> Dr. William C. Menninger

> The joy of living comes from immersion in something that we know to be bigger, better, more enduring and worthier than we are. People, ideas, causes; these offer the one possible escape not merely from selfishness, but from the hungers of solitude and the sorrows of aimlessness...the only true happiness comes from squandering ourselves for a purpose.
> John Mason Brown

> In making any choice, you face a monstrous fact: to move in one direction, you must forego all others. To choose one goal is to forsake a very large number of other possible goals. A friend of mine, thirty and still looking for a purpose in life, said, 'Our generation has been raised on the idea of keeping your options open.' But, if you keep all your options open, you can't do anything. Indecision leads to inaction which leads to low energy, depression, despair. Mental and spiritual lassitude is often cured by the clear intention to act.
> George Leonard

Purpose: Who Has It?

Three descriptive levels can help you in thinking about purpose. Each level has to be mastered, in turn, before the next can be handled. You must discover all three parts before you can fully answer the question, "What is my purpose in life?"

1. The Source Level

Why do you get up in the morning? What do you think is worth striving for? Thoreau probably described about 95 percent of humanity with his famous statement, "The mass of men lead lives of quiet desperation." They get up in the morning because the alarm clock goes off, or because it's Monday, not because it makes any particular difference.

If the universe is an accident, then so are we. If the universe has meaning, then so do we. So, what is your meaning? At the source level we are seeking out and defining the wellspring from which our purpose is derived. Each of us wants to feel that we are here for some unique reason, that each of us is here to contribute to something no one else can contribute in quite the same way.

2. The Service Level

How shall I live? How shall I express my purpose day to day? Abraham Maslow popularized the term self-actualization. By this he meant a certain pattern of action in which you act according to your higher values most of the time in most situations. He called this process "becoming." At the service level you have formed the habit of becoming; doing specific things to live your purpose day by day. You're following the lead of your source.

A service revolution is taking place in many organizations. It has been going on in many people's minds for years, and is now accelerating. The purpose of self-preservation is being expanded into the purpose of service.

What are the times in your life when someone has come to you for help and you were able to give something valuable? What recent opportunities to get involved have presented themselves? What are the issues and problems you've encountered that need your ideas and your energy? What are the special talents you've developed that you can offer to help others? Constantly asking yourself, "How can I be of service?" could be the source of your purpose.

3. The Vocation Level

How shall I work? What are my real talents? Where is the best place for me to use them? What moves me?

Dr. Jonas Salk pointed out that to have a purpose in life is part of living systems and is essential for all living things. He said: "To become devoted to a calling, to have a sense of responsibility and to have hopes and aspirations are all part of being human. To have no calling, no sense of responsibility, no hopes or aspirations is to be outside of life."

Every one of us can set for ourselves a purpose that's big enough to call forth the talents and abilities within us. Our talents and abilities are gifts of life, but we must choose the work in which we invest them. We must express our talents now! What are your talents? What are you investing them in? If you're not satisfied with your work, if you want to find success with fulfillment, take a close look at your talents.

Carl Jung said about his purpose:

> From my eleventh year I have been launched upon a single enterprise which is my main business! My life has been permeated and held together by one idea and one goal: namely, to penetrate into the secret of the personality. Everything can be explained from this central point, and all my work relates to this one theme.

Purpose starts with discovering what's needed and wanted right where you are, in your organization. What's needed and wanted in your organization that fits with your purpose? Complete the "Identifying a Purpose" activity that follows.

For most of us, discovering our purpose is as tough as it is inevitable. Ideally, we shouldn't let a day pass without spending a few moments living in the question of purpose.

Self-discovery is our ability to motivate ourselves, to reawaken our purpose in the face of change or transition. It's finding a new target, a new reason for living, a clear reason for getting up to go to work in the morning. Discovering our purpose is, perhaps, the ultimate risk we must take.

Identifying a Purpose

What needs doing? Something that's needed in my organization (that fits my purpose) is...

Career

One of the requirements for taking charge is understanding careers, career planning, and career management. Formerly, a career was believed to be lifelong. We've come to recognize that life is increasingly made up of a sequence of careers. It was thought that there were definite breaks between careers, and that career change meant dramatic shifts. Now, it's becoming evident that most careers overlap and that we carry skills and interests from one to another. Each career is built on new knowledge and skills but utilizes some skills and knowledge from prior careers.

When the jobs you take are a mismatch with what you need and want, the mental and physical costs can be high. Performance problems can result, advancement is not as likely, personal frustration and stress can wear you down.

Traditionally, career planning has been seen as upward movement to higher responsibility and more pay, or a mysterious activity that the organization did for you. The definition of career planning is changing. Moving up through advancement is only one way to view a career plan. Career progress doesn't require continual promotion, just continual growth.

Taking Charge of Your Current Job

The position you now hold serves two purposes: (1) as a place to express your talents, and (2) as a training ground. In your current job, you're constantly being appraised by people who will have a direct impact on your career future. As a training ground, your job provides opportunities for you to develop and test new skills and to learn how the organization works, how decisions are made, and how to influence others effectively.

If you're new at your current job, or if you are not performing up to speed, most of your career planning energy should be spent on increasing the level and quality of your performance. Career growth is almost impossible unless you're performing satisfactorily.

Part of your career planning must include the concept of "growing" in your job. This is a large contributor to job satisfaction and can be important in determining your need for action (if any) about your career.

Your view of satisfaction and success is determined by your own values and needs. Your perspective on your career is the sum total of your experience, education, and expectations. In working through the following Current Job Satisfaction Profile, explore your own concept of satisfaction and success.

Current Job Satisfaction Profile

Read through the following items. With a circle, indicate how satisfied you are with each by rating it from 1 to 5.

How do I feel about my...?	Not at All Satisfied		Somewhat Satisfied		Very Satisfied
1. Knowledge in this area/field	1	2	3	4	5
2. Skills	1	2	3	4	5
3. Interest in this kind of work	1	2	3	4	5
4. Current income	1	2	3	4	5
5. Chances to grow and develop new skills	1	2	3	4	5
6. Participation in decisions about my career	1	2	3	4	5
7. Impact on the organization	1	2	3	4	5
8. Relationship with the people I work with	1	2	3	4	5
9. General motivation for this kind of work	1	2	3	4	5
10. Future in this area/field	1	2	3	4	5

Scoring Key

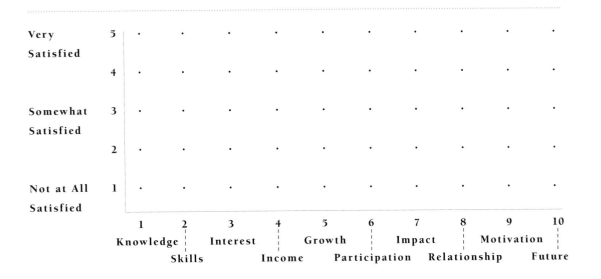

		1	2	3	4	5	6	7	8	9	10
Very Satisfied	5	.	.	.	.	.	.	.	.	.	.
	4	.	.	.	.	.	.	.	.	.	.
Somewhat Satisfied	3	.	.	.	.	.	.	.	.	.	.
	2	.	.	.	.	.	.	.	.	.	.
Not at All Satisfied	1	.	.	.	.	.	.	.	.	.	.

Knowledge — Interest — Growth — Impact — Motivation

Skills — Income — Participation — Relationship — Future

Plot your answers on the Scoring Key by connecting the dots with a line. Where there is low satisfaction, try to identify some reasons for it. Where are the largest gaps between the present and the ideal you?

The Profile is intended to help you quickly analyze your current work situation. The questions are not the only ones you should be asking yourself. Whether or not your answers indicate a need for growth or change, it's always a good idea to periodically assess where you are and to set revised goals. It's highly probable that staying up to date can only be achieved by deliberately projecting yourself into changed conditions.

Analysis of your current satisfaction (recognizing that no job is perfect) should provide the basis for job planning, redesigning, or growth.

The following Network Exercise encourages you to seek information from other sources about your abilities and future. It's primarily aimed at allowing you to expand the information on your own Current Job Satisfaction Profile by collecting insights from other sources. Before approaching these people, ask yourself:

- What specific Profile questions do I really want feedback on?
- What specific Profile questions are of most importance to me in analyzing my current job?

Don't be tempted to skip the Network Exercise or cut it short. The value of your career planning effort is determined solely by the honesty and quality of information it contains.

Use the additional information you obtain to confirm, add, delete, or modify your Current Job Satisfaction Profile.

Network Exercise
Summary of Insights From My Network

Review your Current Job Satisfaction Profile with selected people whom you trust to give you clear and honest feedback. Jot their ideas below.

Their comments/questions/insights were:

Manager _____
_____(Name)_____

Insight _____

Manager's Manager _____
_____(Name)_____

Insight _____

Colleagues _____
_____(Names)_____

Insight _____

Insight _____

Insight _____

Clients/Customers _____
_____(Names)_____

Insight _____

Insight _____

Insight _____

Advisors/Mentors/Friends_____
_____(Names)_____

Insight _____

Insight _____

Insight _____

Summarize Your Feelings About Your Current Job

Which of the following best describes how you feel about your current job? Check (✓) one.

❏ It's a great job.

❏ I'm challenged and growing.

❏ I'm reasonably content but would like to make a few changes.

❏ It's okay, but I'm less challenged than in the past.

❏ I'm getting dissatisfied and feeling somewhat discontent.

❏ I'm not satisfied. I feel trapped and don't know how to grow or move.

❏ Other: _____

If you're unhappy with your job but basically content with the type of work you do, concentrate on finding better but similar jobs. If your discontent comes from the work itself, your goal is to move into a more suitable area or field. If you've found a satisfying career situation, stay with it, enjoy it, do it superbly. But, consider that ongoing career planning is a fact of life today. Lifelong learning and development have become a necessity as technological change and global competition eliminate or restructure millions of jobs each year. People who assume that an organization will take care of them forever are often rudely surprised by technological change, mergers, or competitive reorganizations that leave them under- or unemployed.

You have the responsibility for your career success. Your decisions and actions (not what the company or your manager does) will determine your career growth and satisfaction. You work for yourself.

Ten Typical Questions About Taking Charge of Careers

Here are brief answers to the questions most often asked about careers.

1. Q: What is a career?

A: Ideally, a career is an increasingly satisfying and rewarding series of jobs or assignments over your lifetime that allow you to use your best talents.

2. Q: Why is it necessary to plan a career?

A: By leaving your career to fate, you turn control over to other people who don't have the same interest in your career goals that you do. Also, in a changing economy and work world, job obsolescence is a key factor that needs to be periodically examined.

3. Q: Am I alone in finding career planning to be difficult?

A: No. But, think of planning as simply organizing your luck. Timing, of course, is half the battle. Timing, however, tends to favor the prepared person! Timing and opportunity can be used only when one

81

is aware that they are present. How frequently has opportunity knocked and you didn't hear it?

4. Q: *Can I get help in planning my career?*

A: Two major resources are available: books and people. Books can supply some basic tools; they can't generate your motivation. People can provide feedback on your career plans. Review the Suggested Resources in this section for further books and ideas to support your career planning.

5. Q: *How do I identify my greatest skills and talents?*

A: Complete the Talents activities in Section III, then get feedback from managers, coworkers, friends, and family.

6. Q: *How do I find out which jobs match my talents?*

A: Once you've decided which of your talents are the ones you most want to use, you must begin an information search. One way to minimize the risk and get an idea of whether you'd like a different job is to take on a volunteer assignment with tasks similar to the job in which you're interested. It can take six months to one year (or more) to do thorough information gathering.

7. Q: *If I'm happy in my job, why should I worry about career planning?*

A: You need career checkups just as you need medical checkups. You may need to take on new challenges periodically to keep growing and avoid obsolescence.

8. Q: *If I do the best job I can, won't I be rewarded with promotions and career options?*

A: Don't assume that rewards are given primarily and equitably for performance. The reality is that there are many criteria that determine rewards even if you are doing the best job in your own eyes. Life is not always fair!

9. Q: *Is it risky to change jobs?*

   A: Yes. Risk is the element in career planning everyone wishes would go away. Orderly and risk-free career planning is unlikely. Risk might mean you will be moving from a job or career that doesn't make full use of your talents to one that does.

10. Q: *Is switching jobs very often seen as a sign of confusion or disloyalty?*

   A: It can if the job changes were made with no apparent rationale. The job moves should indicate growth with each step. Most managers realize that the average person today is growth-oriented. The most resistance to switching jobs (or careers) often comes from colleagues or members of one's family who may feel threatened by a proposed change. Human beings are dynamic, not static. We grow and our needs change.

From Questions to Resources

The key to career planning is thorough information gathering. Don't assume that you know yourself well and therefore don't need an assessment process for career issues.

The chart on the next page is designed to help you conduct your own self-assessment and to clarify areas of your career and life that you'd like to explore further.

Suggested Resources

Directions:

Review the questions and possible responses listed and circle the questions that most closely fit you, your career, or your special situation. Review the resources listed. You may wish to explore these relative to your needs. (Copies are available in most public libraries and bookstores.)

From Questions	*Possible Responses*	*To Resources*
Life Planning		
1. What type of work fits with my lifestyle?	"I'd be happier in my job if I felt like I really fit in."	*Build Your Own Rainbow* by Barrie Hopson and Mike Scally
2. Where do I want to live?	"Relocation would be hard on my teenagers."	*If You Don't Know Where You're Going, You'll Probably End Up Somewhere Else* by David P. Campbell
3. What do I want out of life?	"I have a feeling that life is going by and I'm not getting what I want out of it."	*Transitions* by William Bridges
4. What tradeoffs should I make in order to reach my career goals?	"There's no point to do any planning. How can you outguess what the future will bring?"	*The Power of Purpose* by Richard Leider
5. Which factors do I and don't I control in pursuing my career goals?	"I feel I don't have any control over what's happening to me."	*The Three Boxes of Life* by Richard Bolles
6. How can I combine parenting and my work life?	"With both of us pursuing careers and the kids in school, I couldn't even think of making a move at this time."	*Life Balance* by Richard and Linda Eyre

From Questions	Possible Responses	To Resources

Career Planning

7. Which tasks and relationships would I find most rewarding?

"What I want and what the company wants may not be the same thing."

7 Kinds of Smart by Thomas Armstrong

8. What career paths are realistic and achievable for me?

"When you get to be my age, you're pretty much locked into one path."

Build Your Own Rainbow by Barrie Hopson and Mike Scally

9. How do I get out of a boring situation?

"This is a real dead-end job. There's nowhere for someone like me to go from here."

What Color Is Your Parachute? by Richard Bolles

10. What are the kinds of special training and experience I need to advance in my career?

"Career planning sounds nice. But you know and I know it just isn't possible."

The Plateauing Trap by Judith Bardwick

11. How can I stretch my capabilities to their limits within my present job?

"The boss would have a fit if I even mentioned making a change."

The Inventureres: Excursions in Life and Career Renewal by Janet Hagberg & Richard Leider

12. Who should I talk with about career decisions?

"Things have been going pretty well for me. I'd better let well enough alone."

Megatrends Two Thousand by John Naisbitt & Patricia Aburdene

85

From Questions	Possible Resources	To Resources

Special Situation Planning

From Questions	Possible Resources	To Resources
13. How can I be more assertive?	"I'm shy. Let's face it, getting ahead here is going to be difficult for me."	*Assertiveness* by Barry Hopson and Mike Scally
14. How can I establish more effective relationships?	"I live for my work, I wouldn't know what to do with myself if I didn't have this job to go to."	*Making Our Lives Our Own* by Marilyn Mason
15. How can I determine some new leisure interests?	"My life balance is out of whack."	*Life Balance* by Linda & Richard Eyre
16. What learning options are open to me?	"The only way I can change the career track is by going back to school. But how do I manage that at my age?"	*Changing Course* by Maggie Smith
17. How can I plan for my retirement?	"I might just as well serve out my time. I'm too close to retirement to do anything else."	*Age Wave* by Ken Dychtwald
18. How can I manage my work/life stress?	"Something's got to give. I'm not sure I can handle the increased responsibility at work and a family, too."	*Hope for the Flowers* by Trina Paulus

The areas I need to take charge of are:

Life Planning (Specify) _____

_____

_____

_____

Career Planning (Specify) _____

_____

_____

_____

Special Situation Planning (Specify) _____

_____

_____

_____

Spirituality

You may ask why a book on life skills is devoting a section to the subject of spirituality. There are easier and less controversial subjects. Spirituality is a topic about which most people disagree strongly, and discussions often lead to self-righteousness.

A surprising number of people reach their middle years with bodies, relationships, and jobs reasonably intact. Nothing visible seems wrong with their lives, and yet a voice begins to make itself heard that something is missing: "Is this all there is?"

They hunger for

- Meaning—exploring why they're doing what they're doing; "How do I fit in the grand scheme of things?"
- Intimacy—establishing deeper, more connected relationships.
- Growth—discovering or expressing their fullest talents and potential.

To be spiritual is to be conscious of your relationship to the environment, to fellow humans, to nature, and to that which lies beyond the world of the senses. In simplest terms, to be spiritual is to be connected. The spiritual fuses all of life and makes the whole world entitled to reverence and respect.

If you live in a spiritual vacuum, you might try to fill the emptiness with other diversions (work, money, possessions, alcohol, entertainment). However, these things don't bring inner peace.

If you become interested in spiritual matters and begin to explore them, a feeling of connection begins. To feel connected—the context of a whole—is essential for aliveness, deep meaning, and true health. A balanced life is one of body, mind, and spirit.

With a renewed sense of meaning or a deeper purpose in life, the worst tragedies and most difficult changes can be faced with a sense of inner strength.

Many people have had great experiences with religion. Others have had bad experiences or have been forced to suppress a crucial part of themselves. Those with few or no religious or spiritual experiences have had their inner search for purpose unfulfilled or shut down.

When you look at your own life, in what ways are you held back from fully exploring your spiritual questions? When do you feel close to a source of higher power?

Losing your spiritual connection can create a feeling of loneliness and isolation, especially during a crisis or when faced with changes. In today's changing world, many people are going back to the basics, asking questions usually associated with spirituality.

It's easy to fall into a rut that causes you to avoid these questions. When that happens, everything looks like a struggle and your life seems to be an endless rat race. When you renew your spiritual connection in life, you start to realize you're part of something larger than your daily crises.

Resources for spiritual growth are endless. Many methods and disciplines can lead toward spirituality. Spirituality isn't easy. External barriers to spiritual growth include time, place, work, and even peer pressures. The most difficult barriers, however, are internal-ego, control, trust, and even reward.

Spirituality can be discovered through organized religion, in nature, by meditating, by reading books, or by listening to people from a variety of backgrounds.

Wherever you seek answers, make sure you don't avoid your spiritual questions. Reflect on the following topics.

- In your own family or background, who are the people that seemed to have a clear sense of their own spirituality?
- What was there about them that gave you a sense of their spirituality?
- In what ways have you felt uncomfortable discussing your spiritual questions with others?
- In what ways have you been too busy to have concerns about meaning and purpose?
- At what times or in what situations did you think more seriously about spiritual questions?
- What's missing from your spiritual life?

Taking Charge of Spiritual Growth

If you want to take charge of your spiritual growth, there are several things to keep in mind. The spiritual dimension gets at the heart of personal purpose.

The first and most important step is to determine that spiritual growth will be a part of one's life. Once that decision is made, the variety of approaches is limitless. Solo time, silence, reading and reflection, journaling, meditation, and prayer are all ingredients of spiritual growth. Observing the world of nature, reading great literature (with timeless themes), reading biographies (spiritual values in action), listening to music, and viewing art are all expressions of spirituality. How you put them together will make your life unique. Choose activities that suite your inclinations.

Your daily planning can be a spiritual activity if you recognize that you express your values through the daily activities you put on the calendar and the "to do" list. Decide that your daily schedule will include time for spiritual growth. Set aside time; unless you plan "solo time," it won't happen. All forms of spirituality have some form of discipline. The first, and essential, step is taking time. The trick, of course, is to be regular about it; anyone can do these things irregularly. Create that time and place for yourself. Read "The Daily Solo" in Section VI.

The spiritual side of life is never static. It's always growing, showing new sides of itself. Even with a written purpose statement, your understanding of it will grow and new dimensions will be revealed over time.

You will find new ways of expressing your purpose. As your purpose becomes clearer, you become stronger and more constant in your ability to take charge of spiritual growth.

Health

Health is impacted by your level of fitness, as is the process of aging. Although we seem to be a very active, exercise-oriented society, statistics indicate that our youth are in disturbingly poor physical condition and that most adults don't have any defined exercise or wellness program.

A successful insurance salesman in his mid-fifties put it this way:

> I've been horrified to see what the insurance underwriters think of the health of my prospects. Whereas, five and ten years ago they got preferred policies, now all sorts of ailments are cropping up. Sometimes they can't even get the insurance they need. Often they have to pay far more. It seems to sneak up on them as they get caught up in their work and family demands. Their leisure activities often consist of parties and nice dinners. Exercise is an occasional steam bath or playing golf from a cart. All of a sudden, it's weight, blood pressure, other heart problems...

You can see manifestations of this in the way people spend their leisure time:

- On a marvelous ski trip on a beautiful day, a skier stops at noon..."Just too tired."
- On a beautiful river, the rafting trip becomes less fun because "I'm exhausted."
- "I'm too tired to go to the show."
- "Leave that to the young people."
- "I can remember when I could do that..."
- "You young people have so much energy."

Is this happening to you? Regardless of where you are in your life cycle, it's worthwhile to take the time to appraise:

- Your energy, vitality, and condition today.
- How you're coping with your aging.
- Your overall wellness.

Aging

The cultural expectation of growing old includes degeneration, illness, and living a less full life.

Fortunately, people feel better and are more active than in the past. Only 5 percent of all people over age sixty-five need continuous care in nursing facilities.

"Well aging" is a state of mind, an attitude. It's the creative ability to live well with body awareness and sensitivity. It's being able to relax and to experience pleasure. It means seeking balance, flexibility, and strength. It means avoiding toxic environments and people. Studies made by the Duke University Center for the Study of Aging and Human Development disprove many of the myths about growing old. Some of the popular misconceptions include the belief that with advancing age intelligence declines, one is more prone to illness, reactions slow, and sex life is nonexistent.

It is also untrue that older people are unhappy, or that they dwell on the past. In her research Dr. Bernice Neugarten of the University of Chicago found that the majority of older people said the present was the best time of their lives.

For some people their sixty-fifth birthday marks a mental turning point in their lives. For others this turning point may be at some other significant birthday, such as the classic forty. The experience can be unsettling, even a crisis, if you've accepted society's stereotypes of aging.

Our bodies age at different rates, and so do different parts of our bodies. Your attitude about aging is just as important as your habits. Good health depends upon both a healthy mind and a healthy body; it's impossible to separate the two.

A big fallacy is that you're as old as the number of years you have lived. Physicians know this is untrue. Some sixty-year-olds have the bodies and minds of forty-year-olds; some forty-year-olds are so stressed they might as well be eighty.

You have more than one age. Complete these statements:

"Chronologically" I am_____years old. (date on my birth certificate)

"Biologically" I feel_____years old. (based on my vitality)

"Personally" I feel_____years old. (based on my self-concept)

Contemplate your reactions to that simple exercise. Write in the following blank anything you feel or would like to do to change the trend of your life. Do this regardless of your current age.

My thoughts and feelings on my age remind me to: _____

_____

_____

_____

Fitness and Health

After analyzing some aspects of growing older, it's important to turn to a subject that affects each of us at any stage of life: fitness and health.

Your overall wellness impacts not only your life but also those around you. On a more personal level, chances are that you'll have considerably more fun and enjoyment during your life if you have more stamina, energy, and vitality.

There's no time like the present to take a few minutes to examine your own situation. Begin with the following awareness test.

Awareness Test

1. Describe your exercise and recreation program:
   - ❏ Little or no exercise
   - ❏ Walk at least 1/2 hour three or more times per week.
   - ❏ Easy to moderate exercise three or more times per week.
   - ❏ Fairly vigorous exercise three or more times per week.

2. Describe your daily routine:
   - ❏ Mostly mental activity little or no physical activity.
   - ❏ Combination of physical and mental activity including considerable walking and climbing stairs.
   - ❏ Substantial physical activity plus the need to be mentally alert.

3. Describe your eating habits:
   - ❏ Eat meat, cheese, eggs, and whole milk products almost every meal.
   - ❏ Eat dessert at least one meal per day.
   - ❏ Sugar, salt, and white bread on table.

❏ Eat relatively few fruits and vegetables.

❏ Eat moderate amounts of fruits and vegetables.

❏ Fruits and vegetables are a significant part of my diet.

❏ Eat snacks frequently.

❏ Eat fast foods at least twice per week.

❏ Eat only whole-grain cereals.

❏ Eat almost no sugar, salt.

❏ Eat no whole milk products.

4. Weight:

❏ Concerned about my weight.

❏ No weight problem.

❏ Weight is constant problem. I diet and lose weight; then put it on again.

❏ Control my weight by eating and regular exercise.

5. Describe your drinking habits:

❏ Drink regularly and sometimes worry that drinking is too much a part of my lifestyle.

❏ Drink less now than before.

❏ Drink in moderation.

❏ Don't drink at all.

6. Describe your smoking habits:

❏ Smoke and don't plan to quit.

❏ Smoke and would like to quit.

❏ Have tried to quit but haven't succeeded.

❏ Quit less than a year ago.

❏ Quit successfully more than a year ago.

❏ Have never smoked.

7. Describe your prescription and other drug use:

❏ Use a lot of prescription and nonprescription drugs.

❏ Use a lot of prescription and nonprescription drugs but am often concerned about the amount.

❏ Rarely use nonprescription drugs.

❏ Use prescription drugs only when prescribed by doctor.

❏ Don't use drugs.

8. Describe the stress in your life:

❏ Tend to feel overextended and sometimes overwhelmed by my commitments and responsibilities.

❏ Have a difficult time enjoying my leisure time.

❏ Often turn to total escapes from the pressure of my life.

❏ Often feel under pressure but am developing ways to handle it.

❏ Have definite leisure activities that I enjoy.

❏ Have definite leisure activities to relieve stress.

❏ Experience stressful situations but can control my life.

❏ Am seldom overwhelmed.

What Next?

After you've looked at your answers, stop to contemplate them. Then identify the changes you need to make. Overall, how do you feel about the answers? Note what would need to "let go" of in particular areas. What obstacles do you see in letting go?

I need to change:

Exercise:

Daily Routine:

Weight:

Alcohol/Drugs:

Physical Fitness

There are two sides to the body health portion of your life. The first is your medical health. Don't let too much time go by without having significant medical checkups. What is a reasonable time frame? Up to age forty you should have a physical every two years. After age forty have an exam every year.

These are general guidelines; talk to your doctor about a regular assessment program.

The other side is a positive preventive medical program, or your personal fitness and vitality program. The following are just a few advantages of such a program.

- Participate in rigorous recreational activities for most of your life.
- Reduce the risks of serious health problems.
- Look better and more vital.
- Save medical costs.
- Have more energy.
- Slow the aging process, or make it more enjoyable.
- Improve your attitude, self-image, and mental health.
- Reduce stress.

The body ages, but lack of use multiplies the effects of aging and atrophy. Care enough about yourself to control your weight and stay in shape. All this is tied directly to self-image and quality of life. If you have more discretionary time, spend it in an active manner. Racquetball, tennis, or other such sports are therapeutic, but they aren't enough.

A fitness program should include exercises in

- *Endurance* —aerobic exercises like jogging, biking, and swimming.
- *Flexibility* —stretching exercises like touching toes or bending at the ankles to stretch the achilles tendon. Stretch smoothly, without bouncing.
- *Strength* —working with weights, or even simple calisthenics, like push-ups and sit-ups.
- *Skill* —sports like tennis, racquetball, basketball, softball, and golf.

Below are three simple steps to improve long-term physical health.

1. Evaluate your present condition. Have a physical and get a professional opinion.
2. Write down a plan for making improvements, not just maintenance. There is competent help almost everywhere.
3. A stress test once in a while will help confirm you're on the right track.

95

Taking Charge of Health

A few important points:

1. The key to diet and fitness is moderation.
2. Diet. Weight isn't the number one issue even though you might like to look more fit. Nutrition comes first. Eating disorders have become big business.

After chairing an exhaustive senate hearing about the American diet, Senator George McGovern said this:

> The food we find in supermarkets, restaurants, and cafeterias is so familiar to us, so completely integrated with almost every aspect of our lives, that it is difficult to come to the realization that some of it, eaten in the quantities now generally consumed, may be debilitating or deadly.

In general, the conclusions of Senator McGovern's committee can be summarized with these recommendations:

1. Eat smaller quantities of everything.
2. Eat more vegetables, fruits, and grains.
3. Eat less sugar, salt, and fat.

A prime focus for many will be the cholesterol issue, including the ratio between high-density and low-density lipids. Find out how you score in that area.

A change in what you eat, drink or otherwise put into your body can be a significant lifestyle change. A little planning and study can make it very positive.

Don't accept the fact that normal aging means gaining a few pounds and increasing body fat percentage.

Don't accept the notion that our youths are in shape. Statistically, the majority are not. In spite of all the emphasis on recreational activity, many are discouraged by competitive sports.

Let's assume that exercise is tough for you. You've always disliked it or have difficulty working it into your schedule. But you really need regular exercise. Maybe your doctor has advised you to embark on a regular program, but the idea doesn't thrill you.

The solution? Don't rely on yourself. Get involved in a group. Aerobics is marvelous. Running groups are fun. Swim with partners. Walk, hike, bike, or cross-country ski with others. An excellent idea is family involvement. Individuals who exercise regularly say that they enjoy life more, have an outlet for stress, serve as a role model for children or others who look up to them.

The principle behind taking charge of your health is consistency. Consistency works first, by chipping away at the task. As you set up your program for fitness, don't plan anything difficult and consistently follow your plan for the rest of your life.

Do different things that you enjoy. Build in some variety and plan to change things as they get dull. Your local athletic club, YMCA, YWCA, or many other groups can help you. Remember to check with your doctor before you start any vigorous activity.

Talents

Human beings each possess hundreds of skills and perhaps a few real talents. One of the key options in the taking charge process is to clarify your talents, those you already have and are motivated to use and those you'd like to develop.

Although "skills" are a constant part of everyday vocabulary, few people can state clearly what their most enjoyed skills are. This part of the book helps you clarify the skills that you're most motivated to develop. If you want to identify your skills in more depth, consider reading one of the selected references with a good skills section such as *The Inventurers* or *What Color Is Your Parachute?*

Studies show that we work best at what we enjoy. Everyone feels that some skills are more valuable than others. If this is true, you might suppress talents because it's far easier to say..."Oh, I'm really not that good at it" or "What good could that talent possibly be?"...than to value a skill and talk about it openly.

Knowing yourself, what you can do well and like doing, is important for shaping your life/work. Any job decision should be based on the answer to the question, "Is this job likely to be a good match for my talents and one in which I'll be able to grow and enjoy myself?" A career built on talents is a career that promises greater satisfaction.

Creating a Vocabulary

Most of us have a severely limited supply of words to use when we try to describe our talents. Thus, a vocabulary must be created in order for us to name and communicate our talents.

Your talents have been demonstrated from time to time in your life, most likely in the experiences you feel have been your peak achievements. By carefully identifying and studying your achievements you will find a pattern of talents you have repeatedly used to make things happen. The most effective way to elicit a large number of skills from your past experiences is to write some short sketches about your achievements.

As you develop a list of achievements, it's important that you

1. Decide what is a meaningful achievement for you (never mind what other people say).
2. Acknowledge that all your achievements (no matter where or when you performed them) contain talents that are transferable to career situations.
3. Consider for each achievement:
   - Was it meaningful to me then or now, that I did it?
   - Did I have a great desire to do it at the time?
   - Would I do it over again if I had the chance?

Achievements Inventory

Directions: Before you begin, collect ten 3 x 5 cards.

Step 1: On each card, list one work achievement that gave you a sense of real satisfaction. Include big things and little things. Don't look for dramatic or unusual examples.

Step 2: Sort and number your ten achievement cards in descending order from most important (1) to least important (10).

Step 3: On the back of each of the five most important achievement cards, write a paragraph describing the experience.

Step 4: Now review the five paragraphs. In each paragraph, circle the one word that best captures "what made the experience satisfying to you?" Enter the five words below.

The five words that stood out for me in my achievements were

1._____

2._____

3._____

4._____

5._____

Talents Inventory

Directions: The following inventory will serve as a reminder or clarify whether your talents are general or oriented more strongly toward data, people, or things.

Step 1: Scan the Talents Inventory to become familiar with it. Under the column labeled "I enjoy..." put a (✔) check next to the skills that you possess. You don't have to be a world class expert at the skill but you do have to love doing it.

Step 2: For checked items, give one very specific example of how and where you have used those skills. Indicate what you enjoy by adding a phrase that describes how, where, with what or whom you use this skill. (Example: "I'm good at writing promotional brochures for annual sales campaigns.")

Step 3: There may be a skill that you perform so effortlessly and superbly that you forget you possess it. This is a talent. You might not have had to "pay the price" to learn this skill as it came easy to you (or you were born with it). You may never have had to practice it extensively. Check the one or two talents that you perform effortlessly, naturally.

Talents Inventory

My Strengths	Step 1: "I enjoy..."	Step 2: Evidence... How, where, with what or whom you use this skill	Step 3: Natural talents
Group A—Data Skills	(✓)		(✓)
Analyzing/Evaluating			
Planning/Strategizing			
Computing/Calculating			
Compiling, Pulling Together			
Abstract Reasoning			
Coordinating Information			
Synthesizing, Combing Facts or Ideas			
Identifying Essential Point or Problem			
Writing/Conceiving			
Other			
Group B—People Skills	(✓)		(✓)
Administering/Maintaining			
Coordinating People's Work/ Motivating			
Coaching/Listening			
Interviewing/Investigating			
Overseeing/Supervising			
Controlling/Scheduling			

Talents Inventory (continued)

My Strengths	Step 1: "I enjoy..."	Step 2: Evidence... How, where, with what or whom you use this skill	Step 3: Natural talents
Teaching/Advising/Consulting			
Persuading, Convincing, Selling			
Assisting/Acting as Liaison			
Handling Conflict, Smoothing Disagreements			
Other			
Group C—Thing Skills	(✓)		(✓)
Assembling/Making			
Designing/Drawing			
Organizing Space			
Fixing, Keeping in Order			
Precision Handling			
Operating Mechanical Things			
Clerical Skills			
Inventing, Developing, Setting Up			
Other			

101

Talents Profile

Summarize your talents by indicating the two that you consider to be your strongest. Review the Achievements Inventory and Talents Inventory.

My strongest talents are

1. _____

2. _____

Where do you feel that your talents seem to lie? (Rank order 1, 2, 3)

___ Data Skills   ___ People Skills   ___ Thing Skills

Brainstorm your "ideal career situation." Feel free to modify the format or add to it.

Studying my talents has clarified or confirmed that the best career situation for me is one in which my two strongest talents of

_____

and_____

can be utilized.

The problems, issues, or areas of the organization toward which I have interest in applying my talents are

_____

and_____

Talents Profile (continued)

A work environment that comes close to meeting my five top work values of (see Work Values Exercise in Values section)

1. _____

2. _____

3. _____

4. _____

5. _____

would definitely aid my performance. This career situation would be a positive step toward my career goal of

_____

_____

The general level and title of this job would probably be something like

_____

Do you think it's possible to find a profile like this in your present job/situation?

❏ Yes   ❏ Maybe   ❏ Probably   ❏ Not sure

How different is this Profile from your present work?

❏ Almost the same   ❏ Somewhat the same   ❏ Quite different   ❏ Totally different

If you're confused as to which talents you have, get a coworker, manager, or anyone who knows you well to give you feedback.

You can expand and sharpen your awareness of your strengths by discussing the Talents Inventory with several people you respect. They will help you see your talents. (Important: Don't get hung up on modesty!)

As you discuss your skills:

1. Be sure that the talents you identify are enjoyable. A talent isn't worth calling attention to if you dislike using it.

2. Look for evidence. Make sure you're assessing actual experiences, not just something you wish had happened.

The Puritan ethic says anything that requires hard work is valuable and anything that comes easily and does not require hard work is worthless. With our talents, we often think "This was easy, so it can't be very important." Actually, your talents are your most effortless skills.

Relationships

If we had to name what makes life worth living, gives it meaning and purpose, most of us would say it's the people we love: friends, children, spouse, partner, relatives, colleagues. Relationships make the difference in quality of life at all ages. Who we love, and how we love them are, in a way, the deepest issues we face.

The number one issue in many people's lives today is loneliness. A sense of loneliness seriously affects one in three people; a strong feeling of discontent with our friendships affects almost half of us. We complain that we either want more time for friends, would like to have more friends or would like closer relationships with our friends.

What do you miss when you and your partner (spouse, significant other, close friend, child) are away from each other? For example, when you travel on a business trip, what do you miss about your spouse, partner, or friend? List as many of the small things as you can think of. Take a minute to write that person a note expressing the things you miss.

When I'm away (or you're away) I miss...

Relationships take on different forms and meanings at different stages of life. Also, men and women often mean different things when they define relationships. Life in relationships with others is a growth process. A relationship "on the grow" isn't likely to stagnate or reach Inner Kill. Understanding ourselves is a beginning point in reaching out to others.

It's critical to share our feelings with each other. Yet many of us have been taught not to share them. Frequently, one person in a relationship deals more openly, easily, and accurately with feelings than the other person does. Historically, men have tended to interact quite differently in relationships compared to women. Some say that men interact "side to side" with their friends while women are "face to face." Women tend to share personal feelings and problems with friends considerably more often than do men. Friendships for women seem to involve more intimacy and self-revelation, qualities that are often not a part of men's friendships, unless they're in a crisis.

The Washington Post columnist Richard Cohen wrote:

> My friends have no friends. They are men. They think they have friends, and if you ask them whether they have friends they still say yes, but they don't really. They think, for instance, that I'm their friend, but I'm not. It's O.K. They're not my friends either. The reason for that is that we are all men and men, I have come to believe, cannot or will not have real friends.

It's very important for partners and friends to share their feelings with each other. But many of us find it difficult to describe in words what we feel.

Think about a relationship that's important to you. How are you feeling about it at this moment?

My relationship with _____ feels like it is:

Inner Kill	1
	2
	3
	4
In Neutral	5
	6
	7
	8
	9
Growing	10

107

My feelings right now are...

The "feelings" going on inside me right now when I think about this relationship with _____ are...? Circle your feelings.

abandoned	calm	determined	fascinated
adamant	capable	different	fearful
adequate	captivated	diffident	fed up
affectionate	challenged	diminished	flustered
afraid	charmed	disappointed	foolish
aggravated	cheated	discontented	frantic
agonized	cheered	displeased	free
alive	cheerful	distracted	frightened
ambivalent	childish	distraught	full
angry	clever	disturbed	furious
annoyed	combative	divided	
antsy	comfortable	dominated	glad
anxious	competitive	dubious	glorious
apathetic	concerned		good
ashamed	condemned	eager	grateful
astounded	confident	ecstatic	gratified
awed	confused	elated	great
awkward	conspicuous	electrified	greedy
	contented	embarrassed	grieved
bad	contrite	empty	guilty
beautiful	cruel	enchanted	gullible
betrayed	crushed	encouraged	
bitter		energetic	happy
blissful	deceitful	enervated	hateful
bold	defeated	enraged	heavenly
bored	deflated	envious	helpful
brave	delighted	estranged	helpless
brilliant	deprived	evil	high
bugged	desirous	exasperated	homesick
burdened	desperate	excited	honored
	destructive	exhausted	hopeless

horrible
hurt
hysterical

ignored
impatient
imposed upon
impressed
inadequate
indifferent
infatuated
infuriated
inspired
intimidated
irritated
isolated

jealous
joyous
jumpy

kindly

lazy
left out
longing
lost
loving
low
lustful

mad
mean
melancholy
miserable
mystical

naughty
nervous
nice
niggardly
nutty

obnoxious
obsessed
odd
opposed
outraged
overjoyed
overwhelmed

pained
panicky
peaceful
persecuted
petrified
pitiful
pleasant
pleased
precarious
pressured
pretty
prim
prissy
provoked
put down
put out
put upon

quarrelsome

refreshed
rejected
relaxed
relieved
remorseful
resigned
restless
reverent
rewarded
righteous
ripped off
robbed

sad
satisfied
scared
settled
sexy
shocked
silly
skeptical
slapped down
sneaky
solemn
sorrowful
spiteful
startled
stingy
strange
stuffed
stunned
stupid
suffering
sure
surprised
sympathetic

talkative
tempted
tenacious
tense
tentative
terrible
terrified
threatened
thwarted
tired
trapped
troubled
turned on

ugly
uncertain
uneasy
unsettled

vehement
violated
violent
vital
vivacious
vulnerable

warm
weary
weepy
wicked
wonderful
worried

zany
zapped
zonked out

Talking Together

How well do you talk with your partner or significant friends? What's the quality of your exchange of ideas, thoughts and feelings?

Think about the conversations you've had with a partner or close friend during the past few months. Are you satisfied with the quantity and quality of your talking time together? In your opinion, do you need more

- Time to talk.
- Openness in discussion.
- Real listening to each other.
- Opportunity for both parties to have input in important decisions.
- Acceptance, judging, or advice with little sermonettes.
- Other.

Much of any relationship is defined by how two people talk together. Talking determines the growth or Inner Kill in a relationship. For example, does one person do most of the talking? Does one person try to impose their ideas on the other, or is there a spirit of listening, clarifying, and understanding?

Partners or friends might be experiencing quite different or quite similar feelings at any given moment. In a growing relationship, it's helpful to check out and talk about feelings and what is behind them. Feelings are neither right nor wrong; they simply "are."

It's quite common to block communication with another person by the way we talk. Partners and friends need to be aware of these blockages and help each other discover patterns in their conversations that can be improved so that the time they spend together is more enjoyable and alive.

What kind of interaction do you and your partner or friend have with each other? Check the answer that fits you best.

110

Communication Inventory

	Always	Usually	Sometimes	Rarely	Never
1. I listen to my partner.					
2. My partner listens to me.					
3. I really understand what my partner is trying to say.					
4. My partner really understands what I am trying to say.					
5. I show appreciation when my partner does things for me.					
6. My partner shows appreciation when I do things for him or her.					
7. I show interest in my partner's ideas, thoughts, feelings, and activities.					
8. My partner shows interest in my ideas, thoughts, feelings, and activities.					
9. I feel okay about disagreeing with what my partner says or does.					
10. I am happy just sharing and spending time with my partner.					

Roland and Doris Larson, *I Need to Have You Know Me.*
Used with special permission.

Roles

The more knowledge we have about our relationships and our emotional attitudes, values, roles and expectations, the more connections we can have. A relationship starts out with little or no information and a lot of fantasy. As the relationship grows, so does mutual knowledge.

These relationship questions aren't a quiz that you pass or fail. But they will perhaps make you aware of the quality of relationships you've chosen. A relationship is a growing process. If things are moving along at a healthy pace, you'll know more next year about a person than you know today. Acceptance of a person can be a beautifully gradual process, just as self-acceptance can be!

Much of our life is built around roles that we're expected to perform. Role expectations come from ourselves, our partner, our parents, colleagues, and society. Sometimes, the way we perceive our role in a relationship is different from the way our partner perceives it. Roles shift with age and stages of a relationship.

Role Expectations

Directions: How important is each of the following roles for you? And what do you expect of your partner? Rank the 11 expectations and any you add in order of importance, with 1 most important, 2 next important, and so on. Share with your partner after he or she has also done the exercise. It makes for an interesting discussion.

	I expect my partner to	*I expect myself to*
Earn an income.	_____	_____
Manage our financial affairs.	_____	_____
Arranging for leisure time activities together.	_____	_____
Care for home, car, lawn, etc.	_____	_____
Be a satisfying sexual partner.	_____	_____
Care for the children.	_____	_____
Be responsible for meals, housework.	_____	_____
Maintain our social life.	_____	_____
Be a companion, friend, confidant.	_____	_____
Participate in community, civic, church activities.	_____	_____
Be responsible for major family decisions.	_____	_____
Others:	_____	_____
Others:	_____	_____

Roland and Doris Larson, *I Need to Have You Know Me*. Used with special permission.

Listening

The major challenge in relationships is listening. It's not easy! First, you must be willing to take time. The accelerations of change and busyness seem to leave little energy for listening. Listening is becoming a lost art and most of us are starving to be "heard." People who take time to listen to each other's words and feelings make a priceless contribution to their relationship.

Listening enables you to reach out in new ways, especially when the other person has a problem and you want to be helpful. Being a listener doesn't mean that you have to take responsibility for solving another's problem. You don't need to cure people; you just need to care about them. Caring means that you

- Take time.
- Are truly present.
- Are willing to talk less and hear more.
- Are aware of moods and feelings.
- Are not judging or sermonizing.
- Are not giving advice (unless asked).

Listening is the language of love. Tom Lutes, in his book *Self As Teacher*, presents the power of listening in this piece written to his brother.

To Brother Gordy About Your Son Dillan:

Our conversation allowed me to crystallize some of my own thoughts about raising a child. I share them with you in the hope they might help.

In listening is the power. In listening you create the depth of your relationship. In the security of a deep sense of relationship a child will come to know himself, expression from the self can be born. Expression of the self is far different than expression as reaction. When one rails against the forces which suppress him there is no real creation, only reaction. Expression comes as creation when one feels secure in his being accepted and loved for what he is.

Dillan must come to understand that expression which is uniquely him. The values you wish to teach are those which do not need words to be spoken. That which speaks the loudest remains unsaid in its obviousness. Do your speaking through being in the presence of his expression without judgement. Let him see himself. He does not learn through you, you merely reflect his own ideas back to him.

Dillan's most profound learning will not come from what you say, but rather from the quality of experience he feels while in your presence. He can only speak that part of himself which you are willing to hear.

113

If your willingness to hear is limited so will be that part of himself which he expresses. Thus he comes to regard himself as limited.

Allowing.... Listening.... Being with.... Dictating.... Telling.... Molding.... Dillan needs to know what he thinks...not what you think. What you think is clearly spoken in your actions far more primally than in what you say. What you are is what speaks. Trust that to communicate. Quality of self experience is far more important than some standard of performance laid on him from outside.

Be in the open question of your son's forming expression rather than filling that uncertainty with answers that brought meaning to you. He is his own answer. Your job is to bring appreciation and love to his process of unfoldment...his discovery of himself. In each conversation continually look to the quality of relationship being generated. Keep working for the greater experience of partnership. Your tool for doing this is the intensity with which you listen.

Tom Lutes, *Self As Teacher*. On the Edge Press, 1988. Reprinted with permission.

We listen to others to help them

- Talk openly about matters important to them.
- Gain insights for solving their own problems.
- Clarify their thoughts and values.
- Make decisions with which they are comfortable.
- Take action to back-up their decisions.

Who listens to you? Who reaches out to hear you? Who helps you discover your own resources?

People who listen to me:

1._____

2._____

3._____

4._____

5._____

These people form the core of your "network" How many of these people do you need? That's up to you. It's important, however, to have one or two people who listen to you.

Money

What is money? Take some dollar bills or coins out of your pocket or purse and hold them in your hand. Feel the paper and metal. It has no intrinsic value.

What then is money? Thoreau captures the essence: "The cost of a thing is the amount of what I call life which is required to be exchanged for it, immediately or in the long run."

Money is a tradeoff. The only truth about money is that it is something we trade our time for. Money equals time.

Money is a problem for everyone at times. We encourage individual ambition and success as a desirable way of life, yet we often criticize people for having traded their feelings and values for monetary gain.

While money has no real value, our time does. It's tangible, and it's finite. Life time is all we have. It's valuable because it's limited, it can't be bought, and because our choices about how we spend it define the meaning and purpose of our lives. You do not have any alternative but to use time; you have to do something with it.

Making a lot of money is usually not the answer to personal happiness. Making a lot of money or collecting the symbols of it is a huge tradeoff. Regardless of your motives for making it (e.g., time, charity), the results will not be what you expect.

To all of us, money is extemely important. What is important for taking charge is our attitude toward money—how we make it and how we use it.

There are hundreds of books about how to turn money into more money (the best way to get rich might be to tell other people how to get rich!). But even with all the attention, many people still struggle with money matters secretly. They key question is "do you rule money or does money rule you?"

Taking charge means many different things. It means knowing what's most important in your life. It means ordering your priorities, knowing what you will forego, and knowing which tradeoffs will be deadly.

Our culture has come to accept "big money" as a personal value. Graduating college students publicly say they "want to make a lot of money." When we look at an average graduating class, many of them seek money as a lifetime goal. Yet, less than five percent of these graduates will become wealthy. The remaining 95 percent will shape their lives struggling for these values.

Our culture's media-driven values can be confusing for individuals who want to take charge. How do we reconcile our money needs?

What sort of tradeoffs are you willing to make between money and time? Carefully studying your checkbook and your calendar can be a very revealing experience. When you really dig into the time/money tradeoff, you may be surprised by how much it's costing you to live somebody else's kind of life. The big question is "how much of your time you want to devote to earning a living, and what you want to do with the rest of your time?"

Many people, at some point in their lives, find themselves running even harder to compete in a race for which they have secretly lost interest.

Obligations and routine carry them along in the workplace; real interests have to be squeezed into the brief hours on the fringes of the job. Stress generated in these situations has a negative impact on physical and mental well-being. Michael Phillips' *Seven Laws of Money* is an excellent book that deals with the illusion of money and the way that illusion works in our lives. He writes of "the four illusions of money":

1. **"A lot of money will let me do what I want."** Sounds plausible. You hear it all the time from people who are working at jobs they don't like.

You hear it most commonly from people who don't know what they want to do with their lives. This attitude leads to trouble if you postpone what you really want to do in life with the rationalization that you will do it later, after you've made more money or retired. People who know what they want to do with their lives go ahead and do it. They don't make the money first by doing something else.

The alternative is to take charge. Write down the specific things you want to do with your life, the things you wish you were free to do. Write down the things you need to do to shape the kind of person you want to be. You'll probably note that most things require that you actively pursue them and learn in the process. The joy is in the journey, the learning. The possessions unrelated to your real work/life priorities are often amassed to substitute for not feeling good about your work/life.

2. **"People with a lot of money command more respect from others."** Money does not equal respect. Respect has to do with how we conduct our daily lives and not how much money we have. All the money in the world will not buy you esteem, just as all the money in the world will not buy you love.

3. **"I need more money for my family."** This seems responsible. The fallacy comes when we use it as an excuse for doing something we would rather not do. Ask your family what they want. Give your family the choice between money and the time you are away from them to earn it. Many of us who get caught up in this illusion spend so much time making money we don't have time to spend with our families. You wake up one morning feeling that you're working all the time and have few of the things you're supposedly working for. Rather than feeling good about the family, you feel resentful.

4. **"Money is necessary for security in old age."** True, money can buy one kind of security. But another security for old age is you. Friendship is more powerful than money. Too many older people who have money are, nevertheless, dreadfully unhappy. Who you are as a person, not how much money you have, is a critical dimension of security in old age. People who are open, growing and loving have a secure old age because they're surrounded by friends and family who love them and want to spend time with them.

Living well doesn't always depend on having more money or more things. Needs and expenses, as many may have noticed, have an incredible way of rising to keep up with income!

If, like most of us, you don't have enough money, there are basically two things you can do: (1) make more, or (2) need less.

Your Current Financial Status

Which of the following best describes how you feel about your current financial status? Check (✔) one.

❏ Bad. My monthly expenses exceed income.

❏ Poor. My income covers the basics with nothing left over.

❏ Okay. My income meets the basic needs with some money left over.

❏ Good. I have money for savings, investments, and enjoyable purchases.

❏ Very good. I am becoming financially secure and independent.

❏ Other:_____

What is your expected income level five years from now?

_____

Is that level feasible in your line of work?

❏ Yes   ❏ No   ❏ Not sure

Does your job area or field have the potential to meet your income expectations? For more money, what changes are you willing to make and what risks are you willing to take?

One way to increase your earning potential is to find what you do well and enjoy doing. (That's what the Talents and Career assessments are all about.)

A twenty-year National Science Foundation study revealed that those who became rich "persisted until they found work that was absorbing, involving, enthralling." Their primary motivation was not the money but the work! Find out what you do well and do it well. Satisfaction and rewards will follow.

Your Relationships With Money

Money arguments are hidden shoals that can sink relationships. There are often secret agendas that lurk behind money hassles—issues of power, control, and self-worth.

Discover your relationships with money through this test.*

Financial Inventory*

Directions: Circle the answer that best describes your situation.

1. Money is important because it lets me
   a) Do what I want.
   b) Feel secure.
   c) Get ahead.
   d) Buy gifts.

2. I feel money
   a) Frees up time.
   b) Can solve my problems.
   c) Is a means to an end.
   d) Helps make relationships smoother.

3. When I make a major purchase, I
   a) Go with my intuition.
   b) Research a great deal.
   c) Feel I'm in charge.
   d) Ask friends first.

4. If I have money left over, I
   a) Have a good time.
   b) Put it into savings.
   c) Invest.
   d) Buy gifts.

*From *Couples and Money* by Victoria Felton-Collins. Copyright © 1990 by Victoria Felton-Collins. Used by permission of Bantam Books, a division of Bantam Doubleday Dell Publishing Group, Inc.

117

5. When paying bills, I
   a) Sometimes forget.
   b) Pay only when due.
   c) Pay when I get to it.
   d) Worry my credit will suffer if I'm late.

6. When it comes to borrowing money, I
   a) Won't.
   b) Only borrow as a last resort.
   c) Go readily to banks.

7. When eating out with friends, I
   a) Divide the bill.
   b) Ask for separate checks.
   c) Pay and have friends reimburse me.
   d) Pay the entire bill.

8. When it comes to tipping, I
   a) Do sometimes.
   b) Don't.
   c) Do, but resent it.
   d) Tip generously.

9. When indecisive about a purchase, I often tell myself
   a) It's only money.
   b) It's a bargain.
   c) It's a good investment.
   d) He/she will love it.

10. In my family
    a) I handle all the money.
    b) My partner handles the bills.
    c) We each pay our bills.
    d) We pay bills together.

Count the number of times you responded with an a, b, c, or d. The letter you choose most indicates:

a) *Freewheeler.* You see money as a source of freedom and risk. You crave autonomy, are generous, but on your terms. And you've probably never balanced a checkbook.

b) *Hedger.* You see money as a source of security. You crave safety, glorify the predictable, tend to trust money more than people, spend responsibly. You balance your accounts to the penny.

c) *Driver.* You see money as a source of power. You're obsessive about work; you see money as a means to greater fame, admiration, and control; are a loner; you have someone else balance the checkbook.

d) *Relater.* You use money to enhance relationships. You're the perennial nurturer, have probably used money to "buy" love, you balance your checkbook and everyone else's.

Money Management

Did you ever consider your "human type value?" Look at these numbers:

Average Income	Value of Working Life	
	20 Years	30 Years
30,000	600,000	900,000
60,000	1,200,000	1,800,000
100,000	2,000,000	3,000,000

Big numbers! But how much does the average person retain? What happens to it? How well-managed is the fortune that goes through your hands?

A common mistake many people make is not paying enough attention to their money. For most individuals and families that means devoting less than one day per year developing a viable money plan.

Do you want to have a simple money plan that works? If so, take a few minutes to answer the following questions. They deal with how you are doing with the money you have.

Money Awareness

Directions: The questions deal with a variety of areas. Some will apply for everyone, but some will find an area that doesn't fit their situation. If so, bypass those questions.

	Yes	No
1. Do I have a written financial game plan for this year?	❏	❏
2. I live within my income.	❏	❏
3. The significant others in my life know the important details of my financial affairs.	❏	❏
4. I save regularly for foreseeable expenses.	❏	❏
5. I regularly save and keep saved at least 10% of gross income.	❏	❏
6. I have complete records (income, expenses, receipts, etc.) for tax purposes.	❏	❏
7. I know my basic monthly outgoing budget.	❏	❏
8. I have a list in a safe place of all credit cards and other valuable documents.	❏	❏
9. I know about the current opportunities for minimizing taxes.	❏	❏
10. I have enough immediately available money to handle emergencies.	❏	❏
11. I know how much money it would take for me to retire or live independently of my work.	❏	❏
12. I know how much money I would need if I were disabled.	❏	❏
13. I have a will.	❏	❏

119

14. I have a written set of
    instructions in the event of my
    death or incapacity.   ❏ ❏

    Totals   __ __

Scoring Key

Add up your "yes" answers to get your score.

Total: _____

- 12+. Read on. Your plan is far better than most!
- 9-12. Take a day out this month to work on your financial plan. The economic benefit will yield far more than years of hard work at the office.
- 0-8. Don't wait. Make planning a high priority.

———————————————

Most people make simple financial management too hard. Here are some basic principles that will make you solid financially.

1. Budget. Make it yearly and measure your income and expenses against your budget.
2. Keep records. Among other things it helps for tax purposes.
3. Throw the plastic away. If you use credit-cards, use them for recordkeeping purposes and pay them off monthly.
4. Pay yourself a salary. Don't get the "fat cat" syndrome. When you make more than you need, put a stipulated "salary" into your spending account and reserve the rest for a rainy day or an opportunity.
5. Write financial goals at least annually. The time spent will be well worth the investment.
6. Keep six months income in an emergency reserve fund.
7. Have an up-to-date will.
8. Discuss your financial plan and desires with those important to you.

Closing the Gap

Here's an interesting definition for happiness: "Something to do, someone to love, and something to hope for." This seems to make a certain amount of sense despite its simplicity. At various points in our lives, we naturally revisit all three points: our work, our relationships, our future.

That pretty well sums it up. We strive toward an ideal. Yet, no one ever achieves it. Most of us come up short; we live in the gap.

Your ideal self includes the purpose, vision, values and goals you want to achieve and how you want to see yourself. The closer you get to your ideal self the better you feel. The greater the gap between ideal and real, the angrier and more inadequate, guilty and unhappy you feel.

To close the gap, you need to take charge. To take charge, you have to turn feelings into words and talk about priorities and direction.

You need to know that your feelings are not unique; others experience them, the struggle with closing the gap is a common one.

The *Life Skills* four "learnings" help people close the gap. Let's review them.

1 . Change
From a taking charge perspective, the key issue in all of this is all change is self-change. Gandhi taught us that to change the world we must first change ourselves. Each of us has the power to change our life and to influence the lives of others hundreds of times daily through the choices we make.

The power of choice determines our quality of life. It's important to feel in control of your own destiny. This leads to actively working on problems, rather than perceiving yourself as a victim.

Taking charge doesn't mean you have to work it out all by yourself. Denying your feelings of loss, ambiguity, and fear doesn't deal with them; it only buries them and makes you vulnerable to health problems. It's critical to have somebody to talk to and to be able to talk openly. Who would be the first person you would talk to about your feelings? Why? Who is the last person you would talk to?

2 . Purpose
People who have a sense of purpose are those who can take any random experience that happens to them and put it into some kind of larger perspective. If you have this kind of perspective you have purpose.

Your master purpose in life is to be yourself, the self you were created to be. No one else can walk this path for you. You are to be your impeccable self, not a carbon copy of someone else, regardless of their power or status.

An imitation is always a counterfeit, and you want to be an original. Unless you have a purpose of your own, you always have to make way for the one who has.

3 . Vision
To grow toward your vision, you must let go, give up something. You become a whole person, not on the basis of what you accumulate, but by letting go what doesn't fit.

That well-known author, Anonymous, seems to have absorbed all the wisdom of the human species and said it just right. The anonymous author of the following piece knows a great deal about quality of life.

To let go does not mean to stop caring, it means I can't do it for someone else.

To let go is not to cut myself off, it's the realization I can't control another.

To let go is not to enable, but to allow learning from natural consequences.

To let go is to admit powerlessness, which means the outcome is not in my hands.

To let go is not to try to change or blame another, it's to make the most of myself.

To let go is not to care for, but care about.

To let go is not to fix, but to be supportive.

To let go is not to judge, but to allow another to be a human being.

To let go is not to be in the middle arranging all the outcomes, but to allow others to affect their destinies.

To let go is not to be protective, it's to permit another to face reality.

To let go is not to deny, but to accept.

To let go is not to nag, scold or argue, but instead to search out my own shortcomings and correct them.

To let go is not to adjust everything to my desires, but to take each day as it comes, and cherish myself in it.

To let go is not to criticize and regulate anybody, but to try to become what I dream I can be.

To let go is not to regret the past, but to grow and live for the future.

To let go is not to fear less and love more.

4. Priorities

Taking charge is about recognizing that life is not a problem to be solved; it's a mystery to be lived; a life growth plan to be created by you.

As Gail Sheehy stated in *Passages*:

The mystics and the poets always get there first. Shakespeare tried to tell us that man lives through seven stages in the "All the World's A Stage" speech in As You Like It. And many centuries before Shakespeare, the Hindu scriptures in India described four distinct states, each calling for its own fresh response: student, householder; retirement, when the individual was encouraged to become a pilgrim and begin his true education as an adult...

If one idea can sum up this book, it is that life has more quality if outer life closely reflects inner values. That's what it means to take charge.

122

Taking Charge

IV

The Taking Charge Story

125

" For every person who

summons the energy and

courage to live

their story there are

many more who

hesitate, who are

afraid, who plod on —

waiting for some special

moment, for a push over

the risk edge. "

The core element of *Life Skills* and achieving your desired quality of life is risk taking. Risk is your willingness to push yourself or your ideas with the chance of loss. "Loss" in terms of time, money, comfort, or ego (i.e., losing face) are key elements in risk taking.

Your self-image is the controlling factor in taking risks, because you act as you see yourself to be. Self-image is important; when you express your real self, you feel good, you are effective and productive, and you respond to other people and yourself in authentic ways. Positive self-image isn't to be confused with self-centeredness, machismo, or acting superior, all of which are attempts to hide negative feelings of self. It's your choice to develop positive self-image messages for yourself and to support them in others. Sound like a lot of work? It doesn't take more time or energy than living with a low self-image. In fact, it takes far less, and it's much more energizing and fun than living in self-image poverty.

Your Story

Each of us is a separate "story." We're a complex combination of one-of-a-kind factors . Who and what we are has been largely determined by our

1. Heredity.
2. Environmental upbringing—geography, era, ethnic background, education, and other factors.
3. Triggering events in our life.
4. View of the future.

All of these make our lives richer and more exciting. But they also bring with them barriers and limiting beliefs.

Most of us know, down deep, that we have a right to be who we are, even if who we are isn't compatible with the prevailing norms in our families, organizations, or society. We have a right to express our own selves, even if that self is different from the selves of others. We have a right to feel as we do even if those feelings aren't supported by others. Taking charge means that we have a right to choose, develop, and live congruently with our selves.

We can't find ourselves in others, although we can learn from them. We can't always be what others want us to be. We can only be ourselves. Because to be somebody else is to be an imitation or a fake.

This simple truth is perhaps the single greatest cause of upset and pain. It's usually easier to become what others want us to be. But, in doing so we lose ourselves and turn over our hopes and dreams to whomever is in charge of us.

Our lives are made up of a repeating story that determines our actions. This story gives a continuity to our lives that helps us to keep order.

Stories are
1. Learned.
2. Operating at both a conscious and an unconscious level.
3. Developed to fulfill needs.
4. Met with resistance if we try to change them.

Resistance to change our stories is one of the most powerful forces in the universe. It is, however, balanced by our pull toward growth (i.e., creating new stories). Not growing leads to "Inner Kill"—a life of boredom and atrophy.

The idea that one can continue growth while leading a planned, orderly, predictable, and risk-free life is the grandest form of self-delusion. Risking is the normal state of affairs in all growth. It means that you're open to opportunities and change in yourself. Risk also offers a way to put your talents to use.

Some individuals pursue risks for meaning and purpose; others for the love of challenge, for self-testing, exploration, or camaraderie. Many merely want a change of pace or focus in their lives. The stress encountered while engaging in any kind of risk represents a change in story. Whether it requires the development of new skills, or the ability to endure organization changes, the end result is the same—you must choose your story and write your own script. Your story is determined by your risk style.

The Five Risk Styles

For all human acts there are alternatives. People differ widely in their attitudes about risk taking. There are two basic categories of risk takers—*Externals* and *Internals*.

No one who is trying to be themselves will ever be free from external influence. External circumstances will always be a source of frustration. You can't stop an earthquake or keep a loved one from leaving. But reactions to and choices made with regard to "triggering events" will determine whether you will continue to survive and grow.

The Externals

You conduct your life in response to signals—real or imagined—from others. "They" is what is most important. Quality of life is directed by what you think others will think.

#1 Avoiders

Your strategy is to avoid "worst outcomes." What could go wrong in this situation? Often you pick a status quo posture early and hold onto it for the rest of your life. The only way for risk to happen is to be forced into action by an external "triggering event."

You're oriented to tradition but marked by unhappiness. You often express anger at the system you view as repressive. You're often immobilized by the stresses and events that swirl around you.

#2 Idealizers

Your strategy is to constantly go for broke. The sky is the limit! Influenced by the latest fads and techniques, you're constantly trying out new avenues. But the new avenues fade quickly as you move along without committing much responsibility or depth to your trials.

You're trying to burst into the upper levels of the system, to make it big. You're upwardly mobile, status conscious, and competitive. You may see yourself as coming from the other side of the tracks and may be distrustful or angry with the way things are. You tend not to be open in your feelings for fear of alienating those in authority, on whom you depend to get ahead.

#3 Normalizers

Your strategy is small risks, small gains. Prudence! You'll take a flier occasionally, but you usually seek guaranteed outcomes. You're pulled along in risk situations by significant others in your life (e.g., boss, spouse, friend, mentor).

You constitute the large, solid, comfortable, middle-of-the-road group who are the main stabilizers of society and who maintain and preserve the status quo. Your key drive is to fit in—to belong—and to not stand out. You know what is right and adhere to the rules.

The Internals

Internals contrast with externals to the degree that they conduct their lives in accord with inner values—the needs and desires private to the individual. Concern with inner growth is a central characteristic, as is accepting the risk to fully live their values. Armed with the daring to turn inward and freed from the tyranny of externality, internals determine their own way. Internals are no longer puppets being manipulated by outside forces; they have become the force themselves. Internals will not relinquish the responsibility for their lives to outside forces such as society, family, friends, or organizations.

#4 Inventurers

Your strategy is a) reflection, and b) expression. You go through information gathering and risk assessment up to a point, then act. Your balanced approach gives you the confidence to create risk situations. You often have a "Plan B" if Plan A fails.

You want direct experience and vigorous involvement. You have a wider spectrum of values in being more open and trusting, and in clearly having brought your ambitions into better alignment with your real values. You support technology and progress but resist deep change. You're on top and a change might shake you off!

#5 Discoverers

You've extended your inner direction beyond yourself to others and society as a whole. A profound sense of understanding leads you to a sense of purpose in life. You understand that your purpose is really the well-being of everyone and everything for the long haul. You tend to be active, impassioned, and knowledgeable about the world around you. Inner

growth is a key part of life. You tend to be self-assured, self-expressive, and often possess a global perspective. You have melded your external power and internal sensitivity to "make a real difference" in your work, community, and the world.

Life Is an Expression

These are a continuum of attitudes that place people in the External or Internal zone.

Externals, at their worst, complain in order to get the sympathy of others and to show themselves as more just, more intelligent, and also in the right. They complain about everything—about friends and foes, about those they love, and much more about those they hate. It can increase to such an extent that the weather isn't good and everything everybody does is wrong. Finally it reaches the Avoider stage, where they dislike themselves. In this way they grow to be against others, against changes, and in the end against themselves. Externals are their own worst enemies.

Internals, at their best, express optimism, vision, and a hopeful attitude to life. Pessimism shows conscientiousness and shrewdness, and it may also show experience. But conscientiousness alone will never be enough to overcome the difficulties in life; intuition and vision, and risk-taking will solve life's problems. For the ones who are visionaries—Inventurers and Discoverers—it doesn't matter if things don't come out perfectly; they'll take their chances. For what is life? Life is an expression, and to the Inventurers and Discoverers it is a mystery to be lived. For the pessimistic person, life is a problem to be overcome.

Figure 4-1 Risk Styles

	Externals			Internals	
Avoider	Idealizer	Normalizer	Inventurer	Discoverer	
#1	#2	#3	#4	#5	

Programming (No Choice)	Who? Me? (Some Choice)	Programmer (Choice)
Needs Approval	Seeks Approval	Wants Approval
Am What I Do (External Self-worth)	Some Internal Self-worth	Am What I Believe I Am (Internal Self-worth)
Little Humor	Selected Humor	Playful
Idealizer	Futurizer	Realizer
Fears Failure	Dislikes Failure	Rejects Success/Failure Dichotomy
Self-rejecting	Self-accepting	Self-fulfilling
Avoids Unknown	Accepts Unknown	Seeks Unknown
Purposeless	Goals	Purposeful
Inner Kill	Average Vitality	Aliveness
Problem to Be Solved	Problem/Mystery	Mystery to Be Lived

Dare We Be Ourselves?

Directions: The following exercise should help you identify your risk style.

1. Check your current feelings about your risk style in various areas of your life.

Taking Stock Inventory Dimension	My current feeling is that in this area I'm a/an...				
	Avoider	Idealizer	Normalizer	Inventurer	Discoverer
Time	❑	❑	❑	❑	❑
Values	❑	❑	❑	❑	❑
Vitality	❑	❑	❑	❑	❑
Purpose	❑	❑	❑	❑	❑
Career	❑	❑	❑	❑	❑
Spirituality	❑	❑	❑	❑	❑
Health	❑	❑	❑	❑	❑
Talents	❑	❑	❑	❑	❑
Relationships	❑	❑	❑	❑	❑
Money	❑	❑	❑	❑	❑

2. What overall risk style do you most identify with?

❑ Avoider ❑ Idealizer ❑ Normalizer ❑ Inventurer ❑ Discoverer

For every person who summons the energy and courage to live their story, there are many more who hesitate, who are afraid, who plod on or who wait for some special moment, or push over the risk edge! The majority—"shelf sitters"—simply permit their lives to happen without periodic examination. Today, more than ever, we are a "normalizing" society. A social mirror is constantly before us (TV, advertising), to remind us of the norms for the good life, the norms that "they" set for "our" happiness and quality of life. The easy way out is to be normal, forget your vision, and imitate everyone else. As Eric Hoffer said, "When people are free to do as they please, they usually imitate each other."

People take risks to experience things often lacking in their daily routines: growth and aliveness! One can't enjoy the mountain view without the risk of the climb; so, the risk is taken. Many people don't realize that Inner Kill has engulfed them until they experience a moment of real aliveness in a new situation. They understand what it is to be an Inventurer or Discoverer. The stress encountered while engaging in any risk represents a new beginning. It's an enhancement of our life, as we test ourselves at the edge of growth.

Satisfaction can be found in healthy risks if we balance the pleasure of success with a willingness to learn and grow from failures. Rather than approaching a risky activity as something of serious ego-importance, look on it with curiosity and allow it to be instructive. You no longer have to fear failure—the worst outcome is not failure, but learning something about yourself.

The habit of "external" living is comforting. It means forfeiting responsibility for boredom or aliveness. What value is there, however, in living on approval? If you live in a constant approval-seeking mode, true feelings are buried alive. Feelings buried alive, however, live! Approval traps you into living a superficial and disappointing life. Because you don't dare to be yourself, you look for happiness and self-worth "out there."

You may spend so much time living and working on approval that you never awaken to the true joy in life. Life will end. Will you have more than a moment of real aliveness? Challenge your approval-seeking behavior by taking charge of your story.

131

Igniting the Spark

The writer George Bernard Shaw once said:

> The reasonable man adapts himself to the world. The unreasonable man persists in trying to adapt the world to himself. Therefore, all progress depends on the unreasonable man.

The "unreasonable" individual (e.g., Inventurers and Discoverers) who sees things differently is an organization's vital link to change and innovation. What we have learned and are learning from the science of change is that we need to be more reflective about where we, our organizations, our people, our markets, our society, our products and services are and where they are going. People who are taking charge are perpetual learners. Learning is the ignition that sparks new ideas, new understandings, new visions. Nearly all people who take charge describe themselves as "curious," "growing," "stretching," and "laying new track." Learning is an absolute survival skill in today's world.

Discoverers have discovered how to learn. They are able to focus on what matters most to themselves and their organizations and to learn from experience. They often describe mentors and key learning breakthroughs that powerfully shaped their philosophies, personalities, intentions, and styles. Taking charge involves a shift in the way we understand our past, manage the present, and create our futures. Our past beliefs, failures, and achievements make up our "story." The past is a resource and a library of learning, not a limit. The present is the point at which we live; it consists of many options for learning. The future requires vision. Within a vision-driven organization,

individuals and leaders risk making mistakes; productive mistakes. They see errors as learning opportunities. They even reward productive mistakes.

If your life has followed a trajectory similar to that of a large number of managers and professional people, you might find yourself justifying your overall career situation as basically fortunate yet lacking a spark of aliveness. You might be one of the many who feel that something is missing.

What's missing from the lives of many successful managers and professionals today is the energy of growth and learning. Take a close look at the successful, fulfilled, alive people you know, and you will find that they have at least one quality in common—they're great learners.

A little observation will reveal that failure, boredom, and Inner Kill also have a common denominator—little learning. In moments of deep inner honesty, we all must admit that we drive our own formula for success or failure through the courage with which we risk letting go of the old and learning the new.

Your effectiveness in any life situation begins with your effectiveness as a person. Do you want to be a creative influence in your organization? First, get your own life in order. If you do that, you will earn respect and be a powerful influence. As one person put it, when the flower unfolds, the bees come uninvited! Ghandi once said: "We must be the change we wish to see in the world."

You can function effectively as a manager of others to the extent that you possess certain basic personal competencies that transcend that role. When you see clearly, you can shed light for others. What cannot always be said can usually be demonstrated.

Psychologist Abraham Maslow suggested twenty five-years ago that psychology spends too much time studying sick people. It should focus more of its attention on highly effective people and what makes them tick. Maslow's study of the qualities of peak performers echoes the research of many others who have since looked at full human functioning. They all seem to agree on three basic things: peak performers are 1) inner-directed, 2) proactive, and 3) self-managers. This is the essence of what it means to take charge.

Effective leaders are taking charge by developing skills that Donald Michael calls "the new competence," which he identifies as follows:

1. Acknowledging and sharing uncertainty
2. Embracing error
3. Responding to the future
4. Becoming interpersonally competent
5. Gaining self-knowledge

These skills are a good summary of the qualities needed to take charge. Most important, and the factor that really differentiates the taking charge person, is how they use their mistakes as learning experiences. They do this by constantly clarifying their understanding of their own limits and biases by bouncing their views off of knowledgeable colleagues and outside experts. They have mastered the ability to experiment, the ability to fail without disastrous consequences.

Organizational effectiveness depends on both individual inner direction, proactivity, and

self-management and on receptive qualities in the work group, the environment, and the culture. Most great breakthroughs are not solo efforts. Behind most achievements is a team of people who share a vision and risk igniting a spark. It is visionary individuals—the collective self—who have to work together to create high-performing teams and organizations.

Ideally, as individuals perform effectively and help the organization reach its vision, they are also able to satisfy their personal vision and goals. Efficiency and performance improve when both sets of goals are met concurrently. The greater the integration, the easier it is to motivate people.

Taking charge is not easy. There is no simple formula, no rigorous science, no cookbook that leads to success. Instead, it is a deeply human process full of trial and error, highs and lows. This book can help you understand what's going on, but for those who are ready, most of the learning takes place during the workday itself.

We learn as part of our daily activities. Groups learn as their members embrace common goals. Organizations learn as they get feedback from the environment and anticipate changes.

In *No Limits to Learning*, a book sponsored by the Club of Rome, an important distinction is made between "maintenance" learning and "innovative" learning:

> Maintenance learning is the acquisition of fixed outlooks, methods, and rules for dealing with known and recurring situations. It enhances our problem-solving ability for problems that are given. It is the type of

learning designed to maintain an existing system or an established way of life. Maintenance learning is, and will continue to be, indispensable to the functioning and stability of every society. But for a long-term survival, particularly in times of turbulence, change, or discontinuity, another type of learning is even more essential. It is the type of learning that can bring change, renewal, restructuring, and problem reformulation—and which we have called innovative learning.

There are too few organizations within which innovative learning is supported. Innovative learning has often been denied legitimacy or criticized, with the result that many organizations are forced to innovate by external events. These organizations are learning handicapped.

Creating a Life Skills Group

A way to foster innovative learning is to create Life Skills Groups. The purpose of a Life Skills Group is to assist five to seven people with innovative learning, with day-to-day risk taking, and to simultaneously improve the quality of their own personal visions.

Life Skills Groups come in different sizes, ages, genders, and colors. What they have in common is that they are places where people get the support they need to risk new ideas and grow personally.

To start one, ask some people to join you. Keep asking until you find people who are willing to join you and who want to improve the quality of their work/lives.

The Life Skills Vision Group

Groups meet once a week for six weeks. Meetings can be held around breakfast, lunch, or after work. An informal leader will need to emerge to keep the momentum and focus going. Some format suggestions include the following:

- Meet at the same time each week for a designated time (about 120 minutes).
- Alternate responsibility for arranging and leading each session.
- Have a specific assignment each week; members agree to do the work.

In participating in a Life Skills Group it's assumed that everyone

- Is interested in innovating, risk taking, and personal visioning.
- Has a commitment to attend all six sessions.
- Will solo (see Section VI) and keep a journal during the week.
- Will respect each individual's privacy and confidentiality.
- Understands that they are not there to analyze another, but to support each other's growth and self-exploration.
- Is responsible for stating his or her needs and getting the fullest experience possible. (It's not a "spectator" group.)

Get ready for each session; you gain most if you have spent at least sixty minutes *each week* in private preparation.

Preparatory study includes the following:

- Read the assigned chapters.
- Make journal entries on ideas that touch you.
- Do the exercises in each chapter that the group agrees on.

Six Sessions

A six-week group might follow this general flow:

Week 1

Complete: The Taking Stock Inventory. Decide on group logistics/expectations. Discuss the Inventory.

Discuss: "What would it be worth to feel completely in charge of myself and my life?"

Assignment: Complete Section I: The Challenge.

Week 2

Review: Week's reflection progress:
- What was the rhythm of your week?
- When did you feel best about yourself? Worst?
- Do you feel other people and events are in control of your daily work life, or are you in control?

Discuss: Inner Kill and Tradeoffs. Process each exercise in depth.

Assignment: Complete Section II: The Changes.

Week 3

Review: Week's reflection progress:
- Did your risk taking this week shift any? In what ways?
- Do you find yourself defending the idea of staying the way you are and not needing to grow any more or experience new things?
- On a scale of 1 (low) to 5 (high), what was your quality of life like this week? Explain.

Discuss: Are you finding yourself resisting change? How? Brainstorm (five minutes per person) how important changes can be mobilized today! Process each exercise in depth.

Assignment: Complete Section III: Taking Stock. Have the group select one chapter to read and complete the exercises in that chapter.

Week 4

Review: Week's reflection progress:
- What are the risks involved in articulating and striving for the visions that you choose?

Discuss: Compare reactions to the exercises in the chapter the group choses to do.

Assignment: Complete Section IV: Taking Charge

Week 5

Review: Week's reflection progress:

Discuss: The Five Risk Styles. Where do

you see yourself?
- What's one area you'd like to take more risks in?

Assignment: Revisit the Taking Stock Inventory
- Decide on one goal to work on for the following week.
- Commit verbally and in writing to the results you're committed to.

Week 6

Review: Your goal progress.

Discuss: Are you happy with the status of your goal?
- Where is your risk taking most in the need of some attention and support?

Celebrate!!!

Next Steps

Perhaps you've come to this point and are excited about the concepts to which you've been exposed. You may feel really optimistic about your growth so far. If so, great!

But wait, haven't you had the same level of encouragement before? Did you make continuing progress or was it just a quick fix?

This time make sure that you're involving yourself in a continuing process that will work. Be sure to complete The Life Growth Plan. Set up a series of steps to support really taking charge of your life.

Our experience has shown conclusively that the vast majority of us need a well-defined system to manage our lives.

The Balancing Act

The big question when we were children was, "What do you want to be when you grow up?" It was too early, perhaps, to ask, "What sort of life do you want to be living when you grow up?"

The modern dilemma, as sociologist Max Weber put it is, "Do we work to live or live to work?"

The traditional life pattern—education, work, retirement—no longer fits a complex, fast-changing world. The standard formula is changing. Many people are inventing new work styles and lifestyles, forging new definitions of success. Success has different meanings at different ages and stages of life.

Hard work and entrepreneurial vision made America one of the strongest and most envied countries on earth. So, why the search for new lifestyles and work styles?

As we move from an industrial to an information economy, the reasons for which people work—meaning and purpose—continue to evolve. Traditionally, work was a means, never an end in itself. We worked to provide the necessities of life and to create leisure and enjoy life.

Machines were invented to produce the necessities of life more easily. However, to keep the machines humming and the economy expanding, we created new sets of needs. Style and model changes were created. Before we realized what was happening, the luxuries became necessities.

Our self-worth gradually became associated with what we did and what we had. The status people, defined as "the happy ones," were those with the most toys. Work became that activity that men and women engaged in to provide the new necessities.

Our loyalties and our identities gradually shifted to work. "What do you do?" (status and title) became the ticket for gaining a sense of worth. Our work began to govern where we lived, how we measured success, and even who became our friends.

As work has become even more central to our identity, we've forgotten that it was for leisure and to contemplate and enjoy life that we originally agreed to labor.

Life has more meaning if outer success balances with inner success. Succeeding inside yourself means discovering and expressing our core. The quality of our lives and the quality of our work time become one and the same.

As people seek more balance, the really tough question becomes, "What do I want?" "What is balance for me?"

Many people find the concept of "purpose" helpful in answering the balance question. There are three qualities essential to creating balance.

1. Your work should be an area of great interest. Working on purpose means you can get up and look forward to the day with the same excitement that you feel on vacations.

2. Your work should contribute to your learning, your growth edge; this means the work should have within it the room for your constant curiosity. It must give you room to keep learning, to grow your talents. It should offer you challenges that

will try you and yet appeal to you time and again.

3. Your work should be something that serves a real need; you feel that what you're doing matters, makes a contribution to life. Nearly every livelihood has enormous potential to serve people, and you'll be serving people best when applying your talents to some issue or problem that turns you on.

Can you exhibit those three purposeful values in your work and survive? Or do you believe that if you worked in a balanced way you'll be eaten alive? To have balance, you have to begin with the question, "When challenged by work pressures, how committed will I be to living my values...walking my talk?"

If you believe that inner success and outer success realms are at odds, you may worry that you can develop one only at the expense of the other. But simple material success is hollow unless it feeds our inner hunger, a process that's the exact opposite of the idea of Inner Kill. Although Inner Kill is considered to be the result of overdoing, one of its chief causes is under-being...an imbalance of energy between inner and outer activity.

Imbalance is the number one stress problem today. And the two most frequent causes of it are (1) rising prices and not enough money; and, (2) too many things to do and not enough time to do them.

Balance is the need to take charge of our time, attitudes, and choices between the "outer success" of career and work and the "inner success" of relationships and personal growth.

How about you? Are you balanced...succeeding inside yourself?

The many sides of life are meant to fit together. In *Oh God, Book II*, George Burns playing the part of God is asked by a tiny girl, "Why do bad things happen?"

Burns ponders and then replies: "That's the way the system works...Have you ever seen an up without a down? A front without a back? A top without a bottom? You can't have one without the other. I discovered that if I take away sadness, then I take away happy too. They go together."

Then with a wry smile, he adds: "If somebody has a better idea, I hope they put it in the suggestion box."

Burns reminds us that the many sides of life are meant to fit together in balance. This is the natural order.

The Ultimate Challenge: Self-Leadership
V

No Regrets

Many of us go through life not clear about what we want but pretty sure this isn't it! Yet, everyone has dreams. Our dreams or visions for our life come in various degrees of intensity and timing. Our dreams shift and change with events in our lifetime, and with movement from one age or stage of life to another.

The greatest difficulties in getting what we want in life are, first figuring out what we really want, and second, taking the first step. By writing down your dreams and goals, you can learn what you want, and in what order of importance.

Let's face it, the fantasy is always there. Toss the alarm clock. Say goodbye to routines, to everything ordinary and workaday in your life. Build a log cabin deep in the woods.

Strap on a backpack and head for Europe. Buy a boat and sail off into the sunset. Live your great dream.

The great dream has appeal to those in particular who don't feel in charge of their lives. We all had the great dream once. As children, most of us truly believed we'd grow up to travel to exotic places and do unique things. The trial and error of growing up never quite eradicates our dreams. Although some call it romanticism, dreams ignite many of us and rekindle our spirit of aliveness.

Dreams are important. Without them, many of us lose touch with a deeper, more profound part of ourselves. Yet, we often feel that we have little time, energy, or support to pursue those dreams that we know are important.

Like most fifteen-year-olds, John Goddard had a wealth of heart-stopping dreams, starring of course, himself. One ordinary day in 1940 he went to the trouble of writing 127 of his life dreams on a pad of yellow paper. Most lists like that wind up with our report cards in the attic. But his became a blueprint for his life.

In 1972, at age 47, he had achieved 103 of his original quests, (see Figure 5-1) reported a *Life* magazine article entitled "One Man's Life of No Regrets." That article, detailing his Master Dream List, became one of the most requested reprints in that magazine's long history.

"When I was fifteen," he told the *Life* reporter, "all the adults I knew seemed to complain, 'Oh, if only I'd done this or that when I was younger.' They had let life slip by them. I was sure that if I planned for it, I could have a life of excitement and fun and knowledge."

Why do some people, like John Goddard follow their dreams? Scholarly volumes have been written on why people take risks. How do you decide what to do with your dreams?

Here are three practical steps.

Step 1: Ask yourself some tough questions.

The older you get, the more acute is the need for perspective, the need to ask: "What am I trying to accomplish in the years that are left to me?"

Do the epitaph exercise in Section III, Purpose. A finite timetable often urges people to set priorities and risk making them happen. You begin to realize that life is not a "dress rehearsal." Reread the results of your Taking Stock Inventory and ask yourself:

- How am I spending my time right now?
- Am I living the life I want to live or am I the victim of my external programming?

Living a life of "no regrets" requires a very tough kind of self-questioning.

Figure 5-1
Goddard's Master Dream List*

Rivers:

1. Nile River
2. Amazon River
3. Congo River
4. Colorado River
5. Yangtze River, China
6. Niger River
7. Orinoco River, Venezuela
8. Rio Coco, Nicaragua

Study Primitive Cultures in:

9. The Congo
10. New Guinea
11. Brazil
12. Borneo
13. The Sudan (Nearly buried alive in a sandstorm)
14. Australia
15. Kenya
16. The Philippines
17. Tanganyika (Now Tanzania)
18. Ethiopia
19. Nigeria
20. Alaska

Climb:

21. Mount Everest
22. Mt. Aconcagua, Argentina
23. Mt. Mckinley
24. Mt. Huascarán, Peru
25. Mt. Kilimanjaro
26. Mt. Ararat, Turkey
27. Mt. Kenya
28. Mt. Cook, New Zealand
29. Mt. Popocatepetl, Mexico
30. The Matterhorn
31. Mt. Rainier
32. Mt. Fuji
33. Mt. Vesuvius
34. Mt. Bromo, Java
35. Grand Tetons
36. Mt. Baldy, California
37. Carry out careers in medicine and exploration (Studied premed, treats illnesses among primitive tribes)
38. Visit every country in the world (Thirty to go)
39. Study Navajo and Hopi Indians
40. Learn to fly a plane
41. Ride horse in Rose Parade

Photograph:

42. Iguacu Falls, Brazil
43. Victoria Falls, Rhodesia (Chased by a warthog in the process)
44. Sutherland Falls, New Zealand
45. Yosemite Falls
46. Niagara Falls
47. Retrace travels of Marco Polo and Alexander the Great

Explore Underwater:

48. Coral reefs of Florida
49. Great Barrier Reef, Australia (Photographed a 300- pound clam)
50. Red Sea
51. Fiji Islands
52. The Bahamas
53. Explore Okefenokee Swamp and the Everglades

Visit:

54. North and South Poles
55. Great Wall of China
56. Panama and Suez Canals
57. Easter Island
58. The Galapagos Islands
59. Vatican City (Saw the Pope)
60. The Taj Mahal
61. The Eiffel Tower
62. The Blue Grotto, Capri
63. The Tower of London
64. The Leaning Tower of Pisa
65. The Sacred Well of Chich n-Itza. Mexico
66. Climb Ayers Rock in Australia
67. Follow River Jordan from Sea of Galilee to Dead Sea

Swim in:

68. Lake Victoria
69. Lake Superior
70. Lake Tanganyika
71. Lake Titicaca, South America
72. Lake Nicaragua

Miscellaneous:

73. Become an Eagle Scout
74. Dive in a submarine

143

* © John Goddard, 1972. Used with his permission.

75. Land on and takeoff from an aircraft carrier
76. Fly in a blimp, balloon, and glider (Only a glider so far)
77. Ride an elephant, camel, ostrich, and bronco
78. Skin-dive to 40 feet and hold breath two-and-a-half minutes underwater
79. Catch a ten-pound lobster and a ten-inch abalone
80. Play flute and violin
81. Type 50 words a minute
82. Learn water and snow skiing
83. Make a parachute jump
84. Go on a church mission
85. Follow the John Muir trail
86. Study native medicines and bring back useful ones
87. Bag camera trophies of elephant, lion, rhino, cheetah, Cape buffalo, and whale
88. Learn to fence
89. Learn jujitsu
90. Teach a college course
91. Watch a cremation ceremony in Bali
92. Explore depths of the sea
93. Appear in a Tarzan movie (He now considers this an irrelevant boyhood dream.)
94. Own a horse, chimpanzee, cheetah, ocelot, and coyote (Yet to own a chimp or cheetah)
95. Become a ham radio operator
96. Build own telescope
97. Write a book (on Nile trip)

98. Publish an article in *National Geographic* Magazine
99. High-jump five feet
100. Broad-jump 15 feet
101. Run mile in five minutes
102. Weigh 175 pounds stripped (Still does)
103. Perform 200 sit-ups and 20 pull-ups
104. Learn French, Spanish, and Arabic
105. Study dragon lizards on Komodo Island (boat broke down within 20 miles of island)
106. Visit birthplace of Grandfather Sorenson in Denmark
107. Visit birthplace of Grandfather Goddard in England
108. Ship aboard a freighter as a seaman
109. Read entire Encyclopedia Britannica (Has read extensive parts in each volume)
110. Read the Bible from cover to cover
111. Read the works of Shakespeare, Plato, Aristotle, Dickens, Thoreau, Rousseau, Hemingway, Twain, Burroughs, Talmage, Tolstoy, Longfellow, Keats, Poe, Bacon, Whittier, and Emerson (Not every work of each)
112. Become familiar with the compositions of Bach, Beethoven, Debussy, Ibert, Lalo, Mendelssohn, Milhaud, Paganini, Rachmaninoff, Ravel, Respighi, Rimsky-Korsakov, Stravinsky, Tchaikovsky, Toch, Verdi

113. Become proficient in the use of a plane, motorcycle, tractor, surfboard, rifle, pistol, canoe, microscope, football, basketball, bow and arrow, lariat, and boomerang
114. Compose music
115. Play "Clair de Lune" on the piano
116. Watch fire-walking ceremony (in Bali and Surinam)
117. Milk a poisonous snake (Bitten by a diamondback during a photo session)
118. Light a match with .22 rifle
119. Visit a movie studio
120. Climb Cheops' pyramid
121. Become a member of the Explorers' Club and the Adventurers' Club
122. Learn to play polo
123. Travel through the Grand Canyon on foot and by boat
124. Circumnavigate the globe (Four times)
125. Visit the moon ("Someday, if God wills.")
126. Marry and have children (Has five children)
127. Live to see the 21st century (He'll be 75.)

Step 2: Write a Master Dream List.

Now you have a chance to go back to your childhood. Remember when you were asked to make a wish list for a birthday or holiday? You probably put down some practical things and then some crazy items that far exceeded any expectations, but, wouldn't you have loved receiving the oddities!

When you stop to think about it, everyone relies on lists. They're useful. They save time. They inspire fantasies. They get results.

Write a Master Dream List like John Goddard did. List all the things you dream of doing before you die. How else are you going to ignite the spark? A Master Dream List, segregated by areas, follows Step 3. Let yourself go. Quantity is what is wanted. List as many of your dreams as you can recall without heeding the usual time and money limitations.

If you concentrate exclusively on today's needs, putting aside dreams that don't fit in with immediate needs, you'll be living the "postponed life." Postponed or neglected dreams will haunt you at some point in the future.

Step 3: Talk with a partner.

What happens to your relationships when you begin to take charge, to change, to create your Master Dream List?

As you dream and change, there's bound to be a stress on your closest relationships. Your change may be threatening for a partner who is insecure with a change or on a different time schedule.

It can be useful to do this exercise with your partner or even to make it a family project. You might each do a list, then exchange lists. Children can create their own lists. Families can come together around a jointly created master list.

Listen carefully to everybody's dreams. Explore the unfamiliar. Include one or two wild possibilities straight out of your daydreams. Other people may not think they're that strange, after all; in fact, the seemingly "impossible dreams" that you each come up with may be surprisingly similar and open up a whole new area for consideration.

Norman Cousins wrote, "The tragedy of life is not death, rather, it is what we allow to die within us while we live." What dreams do you need to act on so that you'll feel you've lived a life of "no regrets" when you reach the end?

Master Dream List

List every long- and short-term dream you can think of.

Personal

Examples: health, fitness, travel, new leisure or hobbies, school, personal growth, adventure, alternative lifestyles, spiritual growth, church activities, community involvement, volunteer activities

Work

Examples: earnings, positions, second careers, advancement, training/education, certification

Relationships

Examples: family activities, marriage enrichment, type of home, deepening friendships, exploring your roots

Financial

Examples: income, financial independence, net worth, savings, expense control, building capital, kids' education, retirement, specific things you want

Goals...and Making Them

We now move to a plan of action where you translate your "master dreams" and current priorities into a form that allows you to do something about them. The six steps you'll use involve thought and work. In summary, the process for insuring that you'll accomplish the priorities that will keep your life moving the way you desire is:

Reflection

Step 1: Complete the Taking Stock Dialogue Guide and Inventory.

Step 2: Complete the Taking Stock sections that fit the gaps your Inventory identified.

Step 3: Write a Master Dream List.

Expression

Step 4: Choose four major goals for this year (balance work, financial, personal, and relationship priorities).

Step 5: Develop an Action Plan for each goal.

Step 6: Transfer your goals to your Life Growth Plan.

Congratulations! You have already completed Steps 1 through 3 of the Life Skills Process—the Reflection phase. Now it's time for the Expression phase.

Step 4: Choose four major goals for this year.

In preparation for the fifth step, you need to do some more thinking and deciding. Using your Master Dream List as a reference, fill out the sheet on the next page entitled "This Year's Goals."

Here's how:

- Under "This Year's Dreams," list everything you need or want to do this year (next twelve months) in each category. Transfer anything from your Master Dream List that fits into this year's timetable. Think about interim steps you might make toward five-year or lifetime dreams.

- Under "This Year's Four Major Goals," choose four major goals from this year's dream list. *Select one from each of the major areas.* Why only four? So that you'll stay focused. More than four goals tends to distract our energies.

This Year's Goals

This Year's Dreams

Personal
Examples: health, fitness, travel, new leisure or hobbies, school, personal growth, adventure, alternative lifestyles

Work
Examples: earnings, positions, second careers, new skills, retirement options

Relationships
Examples: family activities, marriage enrichment, type of home, deepening friendships, exploring your roots

Financial
Examples: income, financial independence, net worth, savings, expense control, building capital, kids' education, retirement, specific things you want

This Year's Four Major Goals

Write your four choices below. Include a statement of your goal and put it in specific terms so that you'll know exactly when it's accomplished.

Goal 1: Personal

Goal 2: Work

Goal 3: Relationships

Goal 4: Financial

Step 5: Develop an action plan for each goal.

Goals must be broken down into very small steps. The more involved the plan gets in number of steps and deadline dates, the better the chance will be for success. Think it through, because any one step may become the stumbling block to completing your plan.

As we've discussed earlier, there are difficult tradeoffs to be made if you're focused on specific goals. What's a tradeoff? Something you'll have to give up or limit so you can make your goal. As you identify these tradeoffs, ask yourself if you really can trade them away. If you can't, doesn't it say you have to go back to your reservoir of priorities to pick out the next most important because the one you've selected won't work?

The following example shows an analysis of tradeoffs and small steps to accomplish a short-range goal.

Figure 5-2 Sample Completed Goal Action Plan

Goal 1

My goal is

To learn how to speak better and develop more speaking confidence so that I will deliver a top-quality speech at the November 14 fund-raising dinner.

Tradeoffs

I have heavy work commitments, other recreational desires, family vacation, lack of practice time and facilities. I don't want to take time from my exercise program.

Steps to Accomplish
1. Family meeting—tell them my plan, get support.   Due Date: 3 days
2. Design weekly, monthly, and yearly time plans.   Due Date: 1 week
3. Sign up for speech class with Professor Brown.   Due Date: 10 days
4. Set up weekly practice session with Martha, Don.   Due Date: 2 weeks
5. Plan creative family vacation time at home.   Due Date: 4 months
6. Commit to Saturday running group—10 miles.   Due Date: 5 weeks

---

Goal Assessment Worksheet

Tradeoffs	Goal 1	Goal 2	Goal 3	Goal 4
1. Really want to do it?				
2. Have support of important people?				
3. Have sufficient funds?				
4. Have time?				
5. Want to do all of action plan?				
6. Willing to make tradeoffs?				

Hard Decisions

You've selected priorities, identified tradeoffs, and developed a multistep action plan. Stop!

Step back. Ask yourself these questions one more time for each goal. (Write yes or no answers to each question). Do you really want to make this an important priority, one of your top four? If so, commit yourself and move on.

Or did you change your mind? If so, go back to the drawing board. It'll take time, but it's an absolute must. Halfway will not succeed!

My Contract for This Goal

Next, go public! You say, "Wait a minute, this is personal. That's fine for someone else, but I don't want to violate my privacy."

That's your right, but the odds of your success will go down. If your goal is challenging enough there'll be rough times when you'll want to forget doing it. You need a little of your pride to spur you on past those rocky times.

The contract at the bottom of each Goal Action Plan sheet is one way to go public and to commit yourself to accomplishment.

A good recreational road racer puts it this way, "If I'm pushing hard enough to get a time that will please me, there's almost invariably a time during the race when I'll think about stopping because I don't feel too good. Often that's about the time I'll see some spectators. It would be too embarrassing to stop there, so I convince myself to run on out of their view. By that time, I feel better and I carry on. Somehow that's the way it seems to work in other areas of life too!"

You don't have to broadcast it to the world, but do pick out a few important people and let them in on your goal. You'll get some support from them and you'll be happier at year's end!

Goal Action Plan   Completion Date _____

Goal 1

My goal is

Tradeoffs

Steps to Accomplish

1.   Due Date:
2.   Due Date:
3.   Due Date:
4.   Due Date:
5.   Due Date:
6.   Due Date:
7.   Due Date:
8.   Due Date:
9.   Due Date:
10.   Due Date:
11.   Due Date:
12.   Due Date:
13.   Due Date:
14.   Due Date:
15.   Due Date:
16.   Due Date:
17.   Due Date:

My contract for this goal is

Goal Action Plan   Completion Date _____

Goal 2

_____

My goal is

Tradeoffs

Steps to Accomplish

1.   Due Date:
2.   Due Date:
3.   Due Date:
4.   Due Date:
5.   Due Date:
6.   Due Date:
7.   Due Date:
8.   Due Date:
9.   Due Date:
10.   Due Date:
11.   Due Date:
12.   Due Date:
13.   Due Date:
14.   Due Date:
15.   Due Date:
16.   Due Date:
17.   Due Date:

My contract for this goal is

Goal Action Plan   Completion Date _____

Goal 3

My goal is

Tradeoffs

Steps to Accomplish

1.   Due Date:
2.   Due Date:
3.   Due Date:
4.   Due Date:
5.   Due Date:
6.   Due Date:
7.   Due Date:
8.   Due Date:
9.   Due Date:
10.   Due Date:
11.   Due Date:
12.   Due Date:
13.   Due Date:
14.   Due Date:
15.   Due Date:
16.   Due Date:
17.   Due Date:

My contract for this goal is

Goal Action Plan Completion Date _____

Goal 4

My goal is

Tradeoffs

Steps to Accomplish

1.		Due Date:
2.		Due Date:
3.		Due Date:
4.		Due Date:
5.		Due Date:
6.		Due Date:
7.		Due Date:
8.		Due Date:
9.		Due Date:
10.		Due Date:
11.		Due Date:
12.		Due Date:
13.		Due Date:
14.		Due Date:
15.		Due Date:
16.		Due Date:
17.		Due Date:

My contract for this goal is

Life Growth Plan

Taking charge means being responsible for your life. You are not a victim of circumstance, you are exactly what you choose to be. Taking charge means recognizing that the best way to predict your future is to create it.

The Life Growth Plan means discovering your purpose, clarifying your values and vision, then supporting them with carefully chosen goals. It includes creating images of what you want to create.

A Management System helps you to operate every day from goals that flow from your plan. It means translating your vision and goals into specific daily activities.

A home builder starts with a blueprint. Artists draw images that exist in their mind. Composers track notes that exist in their mind. Everything that is created starts as a mental creation—an intention, a plan—and then takes shape through goals and action.

Create a draft of your Life Growth Plan on the pages at the end of this section. Once your plan is firm, transfer it to the one-page Life Growth Plan in the back of the book. Then post it where it will guide and inspire you. Once you create your plan, it can be reviewed over and over throughout the year. The external circumstances may change, but the process remains the same. And from an understanding of the process, you can develop a blueprint to help you take charge at the important moments of your life.

A Life Growth Plan is a life strategy. In order to grow, in order to adapt to the changing needs of our environment, a creative approach is necessary. And that's why a strategy is important. A conscious strategy is vital to every individual; without it we float around in limbo. To achieve our strategy we must plan. Throughout our lives we have many goals that will change according to the age, stage, and circumstances of our lives.

As our goals change during the course of our lives, so must our plans.

A Life Growth Plan sets an overall direction for life—giving us a context that can absorb many different goals and the many different plans to reach those goals.

A plan has specific ends and is static; a strategy can encompass several different possible ends and is dynamic. A dynamic Life Growth Plan allows us to take charge of our own lives in accordance with our internal needs. A static life plan creates a situation in which Inner Kill becomes inevitable. A static life plan means that change will be a cause for stress; a dynamic Life Growth Plan makes it possible for us to view change as a challenge to further growth. A Life Growth Plan answers and summarizes key questions like:

- What's my *purpose* in life? At the end of my life what do I want to have accomplished?
- What are my *values*? What do I believe in?
- What's my *vision*? Where am I going?
- What are my *goals*? How will I get there?

A personal Life Growth Plan sets general guidelines for our life. By constantly referring to it, we choose activities that serve our purpose, and reject things that oppose it. The best goals are consistent with our plan. Our Life Growth Plan pulls together our purpose, values and vision and goals in one place.

Working from a clear Life Growth Plan creates integrity. We are most effective and fulfilled when we have integrity—when our day-to-day actions are consistent with our purpose and values. Conversely, when our Life Growth Plan is not clear, our talents are disorganized and largely untapped.

Human beings have always employed an enormous amount of clever devices for running away from themselves...we can keep ourselves so busy, fill our lives with so many diversions, stuff our heads with so much knowledge, involve ourselves with so many people and cover so much ground that we never have time to probe the fearful and wonderful world within... By middle life, most of us are accomplished fugitives from ourselves.

–John Gardner

This quote highlights a need most individuals have to ask themselves hard questions. Many of these are included in the Taking Stock Inventory. The Taking Stock questions are vital first steps in setting realistic goals.

What is your purpose in life?

1. Determine the major purpose you see for your life. Ask yourself, "What is my life about?" Write this in a one-sentence statement on your Life Growth Plan. For insights see "The Power of Purpose" in Section II of this book.

2. What's your vision? Where are you going? Identify your personal vision for your life. One dictionary defines "vision" as "the outer power of anticipating that which may or will come to be." Your vision is your picture of your way of life. Clarifying your vision should be an ongoing process.

   Identify a five-year vision of how you would like your life and work to look. How would you shape your space and time to fit you so that all your best qualities will emerge? Imagine an ideal work day. Daydream here about a life shaped to your image of yourself in five years. In what environment would your best self emerge? Think in terms of both physical and human

environments. What are you doing? Where? How are you spending your time? To what purpose are you using your talents? Who are you with? Vision is, in a sense, a mapping out of who one is into what one does, how one does it, and with whom or what. Summarize your vision on your Life Growth Plan. For insights, see "Will You Miss Your Wake-up Call?" in Section I of this book.

3. What are your values? What do you believe in? Clarify the core values you see for your life. Ask yourself, "What do I value? What do I treasure?" You'll be more powerful if you are working on goals which represent your most deeply held values. Write your core values on your Life Growth Plan. For insights, see "Values" in Section III of this book.

4. What are your goals? How will you get there? Commit in writing to four major goals you want to achieve this year. Ask yourself, "What is really important?" Having priorities in all four areas—work, personal, relationship, financial—will add greatly to your balance and fulfillment.

   For each area, identify one-year goals and a target date for when you plan to achieve each of them. Make your goals challenging yet achievable. For insights, see "Goals...And Making Them" in Section V of this book.

Life Growth Plan

Name _____   Date _____

Purpose

Vision

Life Growth Plan

Values

Life Growth Plan

Personal Goal

Life Growth Plan

Work Goal

Life Growth Plan

Relationship Goal

Life Growth Plan

Financial Goal

The Taking Charge Process
VI

Not Enough Hours in the Day

167

> "You'll spend your time more effectively if you have a clear map of your life's priorities."

Each of us has only 24 hours a day and no one else can live our lives for us. This obvious yet profound fact means that time is potentially the major limiting factor in our quality of life. Ask any group of people today to describe their most frustrating problem, and you'll most often hear "not enough hours in the day" or "more to do than ever, less time to do it in."

It's not surprising, given the acceleration of changes, that so many people let their days slide by, losing sight of the "big picture" in the stress of daily demands from all sides. You have the option, however, to take charge and actively shape your day. Without a time management process, your Life Growth Plan will remain no more than a blueprint. In this section, we'll introduce you to a process that works for virtually everyone who really tries it.

The fundamental question is, "How can I manage my daily work/life so as to achieve maximum performance in a way consistent with my map?" The stress that disorganization creates often blocks clear thinking about broader goals.

Now your work begins. We've considered different dimensions of the quality of life and the nature of growth and risk taking. Your next step is to cultivate a daily discipline to make your map a reality.

What does this mean?

To work on your self-direction requires that you make a commitment to devote a certain period of time to this work on a daily basis.

While the answer partly involves changing and practicing habits, the issue is also one of personal values. Do you really want to take charge?

Taking Charge: The $25,000 Exercise

Some clear practical advice about taking charge was given some sixty years ago by Ivy Lee, often called the founder of management consulting, to Bethlehem Steel's president Charles Schwab.

"Number the items [you have to do tomorrow] in the order of their real importance. First thing tomorrow morning, start working on number one and stay with it until it is completed. Next take number two and don't go any further until it is completed. Then proceed to number three, and so on. If you can't complete everything on schedule, don't worry. At least you will have taken care of the most important things without getting distracted by items of lesser importance."

Lee asked Schwab to test this system and send him a check for whatever Schwab thought it was worth. Within a few weeks, Lee received a check for $25,000—a huge sum in the 1930's!

Self-Management Assessment

Directions: How do you feel about the need for a daily self-management system? In general, do your day-to-day choices reflect and support your Life Growth Plan?

❏ *Almost always*   You're essentially in control. The points in this section will, however, enhance your effectiveness.

❏ *Usually*

❏ *Sometimes*   You're on a treadmill. Greater control is advised.

❏ *Seldom*

❏ *Almost never*   You're in danger of Inner Kill. Taking charge of time and work habits is vital.

Do your best-laid plans often, or always, go astray? Do you allow the constant demands of work/life to upset your planning and scheduling efforts? The solution: defend your Life Growth Plan by incorporating into your daily repertoire four simple habits that will help you establish greater control.

Simple Time Management— Point by Point

1. You'll spend your time more effectively if you have a clear Life Growth Plan.

   This reinforces earlier material, but it bears repeating. Example after example shows that an individual who is dedicated to a purpose, a vision, values, and goals accomplishes more. Consider the story of Terry Fox, the cancer-ridden Canadian youth. He ran a marathon a day for over three thousand miles across Canada to raise money for other cancer patients.

   Think of the single-minded focus of scientists or inventors who pursue their dream with dedication and fervor—men like Pasteur, Einstein, Salk, Von Braun, and others.

   You say, "But I just want to have fun in my life. Be happy, relate to others, and make a good living." Fine, but take the time to really develop a definite sense of your priorities. The result will be more of an effort to make those things that are important to you come true.

2. "Just say no"...often!

   What does "say no" mean? If you're really going to control your life—to take charge, then you can't do everything everyone else wants you to do. You certainly can't always do it when they ask.

   Universal time wasters—socializing, interruptions, crisis management, attempting too much at one time—can all be solved by a simple "no." A nice "no," a tactful "no" but an undeniable "no." For example: "I'd love to, but I have a rush project that comes first..."; "Another time, but my boss expects me to..."; "I'm afraid I'd do a very poor job for you because..."

Solving other people's problems and needs is an enviable objective, but not at the expense of your happiness and quality of life. Take great joy in it if it fits—if not, "no" will help.

3. Develop a picture of the way you spend large segments of your time.

   A model week should contain substantial blocks of time allocated for things that are important to you. If exercise is important to you, don't relegate it to a position where it may get pushed aside because of the demands of your day; block off time just as you would for an appointment or an important meeting. Further, decide what times during the day you want to work on accomplishing your Life Growth Plan priorities.

   Block those into your schedule. If planning, studying, and meditating are important to you, block those in. You may want to set aside two hours once a week for problem solving. Don't try to solve your problems on a piecemeal basis. Assign a productive block of time to working on whatever issue is troubling you.

   Frank Sullivan, a well-respected legend in the insurance industry, was well known for his balanced successful life. His key— focusing on "dream" days and "dream" weeks. He put together models to spend his time the way he desired, then he adhered relentlessly to them.

   Model weeks can be highly structured or focused on key activities of both that make your time work for you. It's a question of what works best for you. Examples follow.

169

Figure 6-1
Tightly Structured Model Week

	M	T	W	T	F	S	S
8:00	Reflective time-solo, journal					Flexible	
9:00	Get to work and administration					Flexible	Church
10:00	Priority work					Flexible	Church
11:00	Flexible					Flexible	
12:00	Flexible					Flexible	
1:00	Priority work					Flexible	Family
2:00	Priority work					Flexible	Family
3:00	Administration					Flexible	Family
4:00	Flexible					Flexible	Family
5:00	Exercise		Exercise		Exercise	Exercise	Family
Evening		Family		Family		Flexible	Family

Key Priorities Model Week

	M	T	W	T	F	S	S
8:00	Reflective time-solo, journal						
9:00	Get to work and administration						
10:00	Priority work						
11:00	Priority work						
12:00	Priority work						
1:00	Priority work						
2:00	Priority work						
3:00							
4:00							
5:00	Exercise		Exercise		Exercise		
Evening							

In some examples, you'll notice much of the time isn't allotted to any particular activity. If your schedule is too tightly constructed, you'll lose the all-important element of "serendipity" —happy accidents! Figure that jobs will take longer than expected and that a little constructive quiet time isn't wasted time.

Take the time now to review your four major goals. Then, think about the time of your life and make a model week for yourself.

As you do ask yourself these questions:

· Do I have blocks of time set aside for my Life Growth Plan goals?
· Am I allotting time for my family or loved ones?
· Am I sectioning off time for exercising?
· Is there enough flexible time?
· Is there enough alone time?

My Model Week
Directions: Chart your model week below.

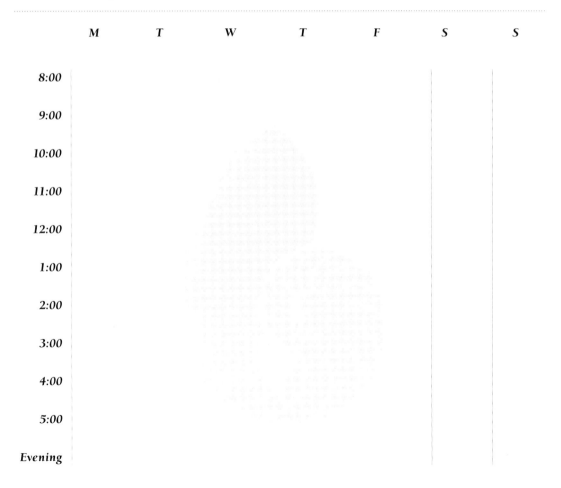

	M	T	W	T	F	S	S
8:00							
9:00							
10:00							
11:00							
12:00							
1:00							
2:00							
3:00							
4:00							
5:00							
Evening							

4. Choose a management system for handling the many demands on your time.

There are essentially three kinds of people. Some try to remember all the things they should be doing in their head. Some scribble on the backs of envelopes, on their calendars, and on slips of paper and end up with numerous notes, files, piles, and memory joggers. Finally, some have one system into which they marshal every input, whether it be personal, relationship, finance, service, or career.

We strongly advocate removing from your mind and your life the clutter that results from methods one and two and replacing it with a sense of common organization that comes from having a simple organizer system.

We strongly suggest that in addition to a management system, you practice these five strategies:

1. Carry your organizer management system with you. Having one book for all areas of your life increases the chance that your life will be balanced. If you have several control systems—office book, calendar at home, etc.—it's difficult to tie all facets of your life together.

2. Whenever something comes up that you want or need to do, write it in a system. Decide whether it's of vital importance, medium importance, or is rather routine.

An organizer management system system allows you to do that. You always have your things to do in front of you or close at hand. Write them down and pri-

oritize. Whether you put everything in the right category is unimportant. That you do it is critical to removing the clutter in your life.

3. Having written the item in your system, set a deadline for its completion.

We all know the value of many of the deadlines in our lives: the impact of April 15 with the long lines of people waiting to file their tax returns at the post office on that evening, final examinations in school, last-minute preparation or rehearsal before a performance or a speech. Introducing deadlines in a gentle and realistic way can open new doors for you.

4. Update your "To Do" list daily. Obviously, merely writing the items down won't help if you don't try to complete them. The easiest way is to review the items that are done and decide which ones you want to tackle in the day or days ahead.

5. Plan the day before it starts. To make each day work for you follow these three basic principles:

   a. Be sure each day has no more than two major priorities or goals.
   b. List the next most important things "To Do" in priority order.
   c. Cross out the priorities and goals as you accomplish them.

As in the goal-setting process, it takes a little thought, time, and effort to set up each day. The rewards, however, are immense. Conversely, if you don't take charge in this area, external influences will inevitably control your day.

Don't leave this section with the thought that we're suggesting that you become an automaton, solely oriented to accomplishing a track record that will put you in *Who's Who.*

We encourage goals that have nothing to do with dollars or job advancement. You set your goals. Having the system will help you to have more control over doing the things you desire. Everything you have "To Do" narrows down to daily goals and priorities.

Figure 6-2
Time Management
Point by Point

1. Life Growth Plan

2. Say "No"

3. Model Week

4. Management System

A Management System

Effective management of self and others is facilitated through the use of practical tools that improve performance while reducing stress and saving time.

For this reason, *Life Skills* supports the use of a management system. A system that incorporates other business tools greatly enhances your ability to effectively translate your Life Growth Plan into practical applications. First, dream for a while. Relax...dream that you're organized. Imagine being able to open a book and point to all the important work and plans and personal goals that need attending to. What criteria do you use to determine whether you're in control or out of control?

A local library gave a handout listing ten questions for selecting books. These criteria also apply to selecting a time management system. The ten questions are a guideline that will help you evaluate your current system, if you have one, or whether you need a new one.

Do You Need a Management System?

Directions: Check Yes or No for each question.   **YES NO**

1. Do I really want it?
Although this question appears obvious, life slips by quickly for many people because they're out of control. How serious are you about your Life Growth Plan?

2. Do I need it?
You may not especially want to carry around an organizer, but it's often a necessity. You need it to take charge, eliminate the clutter, and focus your energy.

3. Will it add something new to my existing practices?
Perhaps the easiest way to answer this is to ask another series of questions. What's your current system? Is it effective in helping you reach your goals? Unless a system provides a new viewpoint or a different slant to your life, it won't serve you well.

4. Is it flexible?
A good system must be versatile enough to fit the practice you're intending to use it for—managing, delegating, leading, etc.

	YES	NO

5. Do I foresee a use for it? ❏ ❏

To answer this means that you must have more than just a vague notion that you might use a time management system. It requires an investment of your two most valuable currencies—time and money.

6. Is it timely? ❏ ❏

This seems like a ridiculous question to ask about a time management system; yet there are new and updated tools available every year. Some systems don't seem to date as fast as others.

7. Is it quality? ❏ ❏

Quality is a personal matter. Answering "yes" to this question means that you'd feel proud to place your system on the desk in front of you at an important meeting. It involves deciding for yourself whether or not it's valuable and fits your tasks.

8. Is it accurate and reliable? ❏ ❏

You rely on the designers to print a product that works. It's been tested and proven effective. The next question is closely related.

9. Is the author an authority on the subject? ❏ ❏

It may not matter to some whether Chris Evert writes about golf or Arnold Palmer writes about tennis. Most golfers or tennis players, however, would prefer studying information written by an authority in the field.

10. Is it easy to understand? ❏ ❏

If the system is too detailed for you to understand quickly, it might not be a valuable addition to your daily practices. You can judge a system by looking through one that's being used currently.

Did your current system pass the test? If so, great! Decide how your Life Growth Plan and materials can best be fit into your system for day-to-day referral. If not, consider another system.

How Will I Do My Living?

Since your only possession is life, or rather your living, the most fundamental question is, "How will I do my living?"

The quest for a meaningful way of taking charge is a cradle-to-grave search.

The unexamined life is self-sustaining. The inertia syndrome is a powerful force to reckon with. No amount of discussion will convince anyone to take charge unless they want to.

The problem with most of us is not in knowing what to do. We do. The barrier is that this knowing remains at the level of belief, and beliefs don't necessarily translate into action. How do you become able to do what you know, to "walk your talk?"

Your education provided little knowledge and few techniques to take charge. Along with most of the skills of the mind, self-awareness and self-management were left almost totally to haphazard development. With no knowledge and training of one's interior landscape, how is it possible for a person to be truly empowered? It's no wonder that many people are suffering from Inner Kill. It's no wonder that so many leaders and companies and cultures continue to create problems.

The answer is deceptively simple: you're not aware of your direction; you lack awareness of your purpose and vision. In other words, you suffer because of your ignorance.

If we understand that your work derives from, or rather, is an expression of your talents, values, and interests, you can see the problem is not one of knowing, of acquiring the "right stuff." Rather, it's one of self-management, of reaching to your core to express our own truths. Self-study brings personal awareness, which brings self-discipline, which brings about taking charge.

You must begin with self-study. Most important, you must become aware of and experience directly your own spirit in the workplace and in your lifestyle.

Without reflection and expression of your core, without specific methods and tools by which to transform yourself, it's difficult if not impossible to transform your company. You need to experience the spirit and power of the talents that lie within.

Taking charge begins when you cease to see yourself as isolated and competing with others and begin to identify with others on common ground.

True awareness requires even a further step, a further maturity and growth, an identification that goes beyond humanity to all of nature.

Time is regarded as money. You're urged to exploit every minute and to use several of your five senses at a time. Such "two-fers" as dialing and driving, watching and eating, jogging and listening to tapes have become symbols for people who are considered well-organized and efficient.

Business comes with its own technology— voice mail, split-screen television, car phones, home exercise devices (with newspaper stands), etc. The "business of business" is huge. There's even a course offered at one university that teaches students several languages at the same time.

We seem to think that if only we were more organized we could squeeze at least two lifetimes into one. Instead of making priorities, we think we can make time. What's behind some of this is the true passion of the times: a lust for more.

Laurence Shames' book, *The Hunger for More: Searching for Values in an Age of Greed* states:

> The frontier, as reality and symbol, is
> what has shaped the American way of

doing things and the American sense of what's worth doing.... More money, more tokens of success—there will always be people for whom those are adequate goals, but those people are no longer setting the tone for all of us.

There's a new sort of "more" at hand. More appreciation of good things beyond the marketplace, more insistence on fairness, more attention to purpose, more determination truly to choose a life, and not a lifestyle, for oneself.

Taking charge is about planning a life worth living. Taking charge is a self-confrontation. It's creating a destination crisis for yourself. It requires the renewal of basic values, boundaries, and directions.

How will I do my living? Society provides you with many reasons for living outside your values, with many directives of what you should be. When you perform well, who are you trying to please? When you're hurrying, is it even at the cost of something more important?

Our questions inevitably become one: "What's worth doing with my time?" What are the conditions under which it's possible for me to be whole? What were those moments when I was whole? You will find that many of those moments were quite simple and had little to do with the way you spent much of your time.

If you could identify the conditions under which your life was fulfilling, you could, perhaps, create the lifestyle tone you want in the future. The idea of "muscle tone" captures the essence referred to as lifestyle tone—mind, body, spirit aliveness. When body, mind, and spirit are all in harmony, you are alive. When they're not, you're in various stages of death, Inner Kill.

Lifestyle tone is usually first felt in the body. While the mind plays tricks, the body never lies. Alexander Lowen expresses this idea in, *The Betrayal of the Body* as follows.

A person experiences the reality of the world only through his body. If the body is relatively unalive, a person's impressions and responses are diminished. The more alive the body is, the more vividly does he perceive reality and the more actively does he respond to it. We have all experienced the fact that when we feel particularly good and alive, we perceive the world more sharply...the aliveness of the body denotes its capacity for feeling. In the absence of feeling, the body goes dead insofar as its ability to be impressed by or respond to situations is concerned. The emotionally dead person is turned inward: thoughts and fantasies replace feelings and actions; images compensate for the loss of reality.... It is the body that melts with love, freezes with fear, trembles in anger, and reaches for warmth and contact. Apart from the body, these words are poetic images. Experienced in the body, they have a reality that gives meaning to existence.

Taking charge is essentially an invitation to define our own lifestyle tone, to go back, perhaps, to the basics of what makes life most alive. In everyday experience, taking charge means not getting stuck in a victim point of view. It means being free in your situation rather than dependent on it.

Taking charge means investing yourself more fully in the creation of your experiences. It's learning to see the world through the eyes of your purpose.

The principal work of taking charge is the creation of purpose, to make life more whole, so that the parts balance. Justice William O. Douglas used to describe what is meant here when he wrote: "Man is whole when he is in tune with the winds, the stars, and the hills as well as with his neighbors. Being in tune with the apartment or the community is part of the secret. Being in tune with the universe is the whole secret."

The Daily Solo

The Daily Solo is like the eye of a hurricane, a quiet place at the center of life, a protected pause amidst our busyness during which we can quietly reappraise the quality of our lives.

The factors involved in human growth are primarily subjective feelings, states of mind and states of emotion. These factors come and go with varying degrees of clarity. Yet, they're ever present and working within us. The Solo gives us the time and a process for reflecting on and expressing our growth throughout our life.

We live in an imperfect world full of imperfect people. In the real world, people get tired and make mistakes. People suffer stress and become sick. They react poorly to pressure. Periodically we need to give ourselves time and quiet to sit and let our core catch up to us, to listen to the still, small voice inside. It's only as we turn toward solitude that the truth becomes apparent. Through a Daily Solo, you renew energy and vision so that you can once again guide your day-to-day decisions. Slowly you start discerning what part of your busyness is an expression of our real values.

Make some solo time for yourself each day to reflect on your Life Growth Plan. Isolate yourself from all distractions for at least fifteen

minutes, preferably at the same time each day. Schedule the fifteen minutes right on your calendar. Do it at the start of each day.

Your solo time is for visualizing the unfolding day, focusing on the "big picture" of what is most important to you this day.

Though it may not seem so, you are not indispensable. Your colleagues at work or family at home can get along quite well without you for fifteen minutes. If scheduling is a problem, practice "mind over mattress" by getting up fifteen minutes early to focus your mind for the day. As the first hour of the day goes, so goes the day!

You'll discipline yourself to live better by becoming more mindful. A daily fifteen-minute Solo can dramatically affect the quality of the other twenty-three hours and forty-five minutes. Often, we tend to race through the day, not really tasting, smelling, seeing, feeling, or hearing. And most of all, not listening to ourselves.

"Time is the currency of life"...and a Daily Solo helps us appreciate the full value of our currency!

The Solo serves as a laboratory in which you explore the possibilities of your life and creatively shape your day.

At the beginning of your Solo each day, examine how you want your day to look. Spend the first ten minutes in deep relaxation and silence. Picture yourself in specific situations. What are your priorities this day? Consider each part of your Life Growth Plan.

Reread this year's four major goals regularly. Can you picture how your daily life can reflect these? What are your two major priorities for today?

When and Where

The Solo works best at the same time exercise works best—when the stomach is empty. Right before breakfast is a fine time. The calming effect can set a relaxed, positive tone that may last throughout the day. It'll affect the way you respond to the challenges of your life. The least recommended time would be right after eating.

In a Solo, you begin to integrate yourself, rather than losing integration. That's because you're tapping into more elements of your total personality, broadening your perspective on yourself and the world, and thereby becoming more in control of your life.

Knowing that a Solo process helps bring about results won't do a thing by itself. You've got to sit down and do it. If, like most people, you lead a busy life and don't schedule a "Solo time" regularly, you may find that you don't do it enough to create any positive change in your life.

Steps in a Daily Solo

The daily solo is a two-step process: relaxation and visualization.

Step 1: Relaxation

Get into a "receptive state." For visualization to happen, you need at least a little relaxation at the beginning, which is often the greatest challenge for many people.

a) Sit in a comfortable chair, both feet on the floor, uncrossed, hands lying relaxed on your lap. If you wish, you may also lie on your back on a flat, comfortable but firm surface.

b) Close your eyes. Take a deep breath. Hold your breath for a moment; exhale slowly. Do this three times or more. Allow your body to become more and more fully relaxed.

c) Take several slow, deep breaths, breathing from your abdomen. Breathe in and out through your nose, taking breaths that are long and slow. Silently to yourself, count "one" as you inhale and "two" as you exhale. Do this over and over again with each breath cycle for several minutes. Concentrate on the numbers one and two, saying them to yourself with each breath cycle. The idea is to clear your mind. Most of us feel controlled by the thoughts that constantly pop into our minds. Visualize your thoughts as clouds floating toward you, floating freely into your mind, and then floating out of your mind again. Keep going back to counting your breaths. It will become easier as you practice.

d) Pay attention to your body. Where do you feel tension or stress? Inhale and then imagine as you exhale that you are sending your breath to that part of your body that you wish to relax. Do this for each stressful area of your body. Your body will do the rest.

Now breathe normally. Breathe in a comfortable, natural rhythm.

The next step, visualization, starts after you've created a relaxed mind and body.

Step 2: Visualization

To creatively shape your life it's important to develop the technique of visualization.

Visualization is easy to learn but you must be patient. You must devote time to it; don't expect results overnight. If you persist, you'll be able to experience far more inner peace than you ever dreamed.

Visualization in its many forms is a universal way to reach the subconscious mind with messages. Essentially, it involves convincing yourself of your strength by freeing yourself of distraction and fears and by getting to your conscious self through your subconscious self.

Almost every culture has in its own way stumbled upon this tool by exploring deep layers of consciousness. Deep prayer, biofeedback, meditation, and positive thinking all begin with visualization. It's all a matter of getting yourself into a receptive state.

When achieved, you're relaxed enough to allow yourself to heed your own suggestions, where the inner mind can concentrate on messages you put there. The normal chatter of the waking mind is temporarily quiet; there is less stress and greater sensitivity. Self-diagnosis, self-healing, habit modification, and goal achievement are all within your grasp.

The Daily Solo depends on your ability to visualize your Life Growth Plan, in your mind's eye. Because of the large size of the visual cortex in the brain, the ability to visualize is a powerful tool for activating mental energy. It's like the lens that gathers the light of the sun and focuses it on a single point. Learning to focus mental energy is like being able to burn a hole through a piece of paper with a magnifying glass.

Everyone can learn to visualize. Visualization means talking to yourself silently in a soft but firm tone. We can control and use thoughts for our own growth and fulfillment. We can become directors of the movies we create in our minds.

When we experiment, we find that we actually program our experiences through our thoughts. Our thoughts are the blueprints for the structure of our lives. If we're about to undertake a new venture, why not use the best blueprint possible?

Here's an example of the ways we use our mind's eye to look at an important upcoming meeting.

Destructive Visualization: I see myself having difficulty with the meeting, being tense and being rejected by several difficult participants.

Fantasy: I see myself breezing through the meeting with no obstacles and getting an easy "go ahead."

Creative Visualization: I see myself listening carefully to the participant's questions and feeling good about my answers. I'm glad that I took the time to prepare, since without preparation, I wouldn't know the answers. I see myself getting the "go ahead" despite some momentary roadblocks.

Destructive images create worry and tension. Fantasy creates anxiety when the fantasy isn't fulfilled. Creative images create a feeling of calmness about the upcoming situation and also reinforce the importance of preparation.

Visualizations can be used effectively in creating your life strategy. The more we use our minds in a creative way, the more our quality of life improves.

There's an old saying that a glass of water at its halfway mark is both half full and half empty. Both ways of describing the glass are true. So why not focus on the positive?

Your attitude toward practicing a Daily Solo should be as matter-of-fact as brushing your teeth in the morning. Brushing has become an automatic process that you probably don't think much about while you're doing it. You execute this task in a routine way, and you expect that sometime you'll reap benefits (prevent tooth and gum disease).

The Solo technique might not have any dramatic, immediate effect, except to make you feel more refreshed after the first session. The long-term quality-of-life benefits, on the other hand, will become quite evident after you've practiced the technique consistently over several weeks. The inner capacity to increase your mental powers in your life will accelerate.

Solo and Purpose

You may think about getting involved in something meaningful, yet the time-pressures of your daily commitments make those involvements unlikely. You rationalize by saying, "I'd get involved if I had the time" or "I'll take that on later."

The Solo is a way to deal with the postponement issue. Instead of waiting until the perfect time to do something purposeful, begin to look at it as an integral part of your daily schedule. Each day you can set aside fifteen minutes to follow through on the good ideas you've had about things that matter to you.

Use that Solo time to write a note, make a call, brainstorm a solution or just do something to make a difference in one person's life. Or use that fifteen minutes to catch up on the reading or preparation work that focuses on your interest or issue.

Rather than seeing purpose as a duty or burden, begin to enjoy it as an integral part of your daily life.

If you set aside fifteen minutes a day to do things that are of service to the people and issues you most care about, you'll be amazed at how much you can accomplish. And, you'll be

rewarded on an emotional level far in excess of the dollar value of your time.

Inner Peace

If you master the Solo process (relaxation and visualization), it may be possible to come upon that elusive quality that has been called "inner peace." Occasionally we meet people with this rare quality. It's usually not something they were born with, but that they learned through consciously living with awareness and focus. They may occasionally become disturbed by triggering events, but underneath it all there's something rich, solid, and unshakable. That feeling projects itself and is readily felt by others.

The movement toward inner peace is actually the natural evolution toward full psychological maturity. You'll find that in the process of "Soloing" you discover a part of yourself that you've never fully appreciated before—a stronger sense of meaning and purpose in your life.

The Eight-Step Daily Solo
Relax

1. Sit quietly in a comfortable position.
2. Close your eyes.
3. Relax with your breath. (Become aware of your breathing, and breath very slowly and naturally. Repeat "one" as you inhale, "two" as you exhale).
4. Feel your tensions dropping away.

Visualize

5. Visualize a situation that you're concerned about in your upcoming day.
6. Three times in a row, picture the situation

the way you would like it to happen.

7. Slowly come back to the present and your surroundings.

8. Write out the highlights of the positive situation as you saw it in your mind's eye. You have just consciously taken a journey into your mind's eye. How do you feel after imagining yourself in that scene? Did you experience it as if you were there? Are you more calm and relaxed than before? Probably so.

Life Growth Plan

To get the maximum benefit out of the Eight-Step Daily Solo technique, tailor it to your personal Life Growth Plan. By visualizing and journaling about it, you'll activate your beliefs in a way that will also have a profound effect. The more your plan is integrated into the Daily Solo, the greater your chances of living it on a day-to-day basis.

Most religions stress the importance of an inspired literature from God (Bible, Koran, Bhagavad-Gita, etc.). Most major faiths and many philosophical systems have found great benefits from meditative and journal practices.

As you sit quietly, picture yourself living out a key belief or value in an upcoming situation. Record the highlights in your journal. Or read an inspiring quotation or passage and reflect on it when writing in your journal.

Some people visualize in terms of goals for the day. Others picture feelings they would like to maintain throughout the day or in specific situations. Others image specific relationships with significant people they will meet.

Some examples of pictures include the following:

- Seeing the purpose you live by in action during the day.
- Moving forward on an important goal.
- Rehearsing a sales call in your mind.
- Visualizing yourself successfully giving a speech.
- Maintaining a calm composure during an important meeting.
- Visualizing a happy "reentry" at the end of the day back into your home with your children and spouse.
- Successfully overcoming the objections of a major client.
- Artfully handling a conflict between two key employees.
- Bravely standing up for a purpose you believe in (in the face of stern resistance).
- Actively listening to your spouse or friend describe the tribulations of the day.

Try investing five minutes of your time visualizing. It's most effective to work on just one or two pictures per session. Mentally picture the desired behavior in detail. Make it valid and visual. Step outside yourself and watch yourself doing it. Suggest some positive, rewarding experience as a benefit from the new behavior. Focusing on a picture in your mind's eye can be quite powerful.

Since visualizations only have a life span of about thirty-six hours, you'll need to repeat this process daily, until you've truly changed your behavior or reached your goal.

As an analogy, any of the buildings we see around us existed first in the mind of the architect. First they were visualized, then put on paper, and finally the image became wood and concrete and steel.

Visualization is a fantastic aid in creating new patterns of behavior as well as new structures. It can be a most effective tool right before a period of maximum effort. Olympic athletes do this all the time. Make use of it whenever the situation demands.

Jack Nicklaus has often talked of picturing the path of every shot before he hits it; great basketball and hockey players spend an hour or more imaging every movement from the time they enter the locker room.

The Journal

The journal is a place where reflection can take shape. It's a place where "inner conversation" or "negotiations" with yourself can take place in a regular and organized fashion. It's a place where blinding flashes and new ideas can be recorded and built upon, a place to gain insight to picture and/or reflect on your day. It's a continuous check on your quality of life.

Journals have been around almost as long as humans. It's impressive to observe the number of people in other cultures and in other periods of history who have kept journals to meet various needs in their lives. Journals have been found on cave walls, on the outside of Native American tepees, and on the ships of the early explorers.

The journal has also played a particularly important role in the history of religion and whenever the quality of inner experience has been valued such as with artists, novelists and therapists. Individuals throughout recorded time have used the journal as a means of measuring progress along a particular path.

The use of a private journal is exceedingly common whenever people have a fixed goal. Journals are often used specifically in situations where an individual is having difficulty in attaining a goal. The journal becomes a self-testing device.

The journal is a continuous program of inner discipline. When you write in a journal, you're not composing an essay, only recording the unedited expressions of your inner experience. You write in it day by day as much as possible to keep yourself in an ongoing relationship with whatever is taking place inside yourself.

The mind is always talking to itself, keeping up a perpetual commentary about life, feelings, fears, joys, and other people. This "self-talk" influences your thoughts and feelings about what's going on in your life. These commentaries create everything that happens to us. In a more fundamental sense we recognize that the essence lies not in the events of our lives but in our inner relationship to those events.

Very often the self-talk can create negative performance. Part of the reason is that our mind is just playing a continuous, unedited tape of our feelings. By taking the time to really put some of these thoughts on paper a more constructive process begins.

Journaling helps you to observe your inner conversation more objectively. It gathers into one accessible place many facets of yourself. A journal is a mirror. It's a good listener, a tool for self-guidance, a road map of growth.

There are many creative ways to use a journal.

- Recording and daily monitoring of goals (work, financial, relationship, diet, exercise, etc.)

- Reading from inspirational and uplifting books or tapes.
- Collecting and regular reviewing of quotes, sayings and philosophies that are meaningful and inspiring to you.
- Road map of your spiritual search.
- Scrapbook for collecting and developing new ideas.
- Dialoging with yourself about situations that caused you problems in the past.
- Inner negotiation on difficult issues.
- Planning future directions.
- Writing down your feelings and reactions at this point in time.

By listening to yourself and writing what you hear, you'll become more consciously aware of the deeper levels of experience. The result, after consistent use, is that you'll see the patterns and themes in your life, the values you act on, the interpersonal games you play, and the illusions you cling to.

There are no fixed rules for journal writing. Develop your own style. It's not a place to condemn nor judge, but a place to observe. Pay no attention at all to your "style" of writing. Write in your everyday language, letting the flow of words happen without censorship.

Think about something in your upcoming day that you're hopeful about. Close your eyes for a moment and picture the situation or event exactly the way you're anticipating it will happen. How do you feel?

Perhaps you weren't aware that you have mental images when you think, worry, or plan. That's because you generally don't pay attention to your thoughts. They come in and out of your mind continually, and you take them for granted.

To begin to cultivate the journal habit follow the same basic format as the Eight-Step Daily Solo process.

Beginning the Journal
Relax

1. Sit quietly in a comfortable position.
2. Close your eyes.
3. Relax with your breath. (Become aware of your breathing, and breathe very slowly and naturally. Repeat "one" as you inhale, "two" as you exhale).
4. Feel your tensions dropping away.
5. Use a journal or notebook or create a Journal Section in your management system for reflection during your Solo.
6. Think about the day you are experiencing or have just had. At the beginning channel your thoughts in this way: What did I hope would happen today? How do I feel about what did happen? What did I learn today?
7. Write your observations down—expand on them. Get in touch with other feelings and thoughts you have.

Some never go back to read in their journals. Others reread continuously to get a feeling of trends in their life. They use this as a tool to decide it's time to make decisions. They use it to monitor their goal setting and goal achievement process.

Daily Habits

A journal is also an opportunity for you to establish and/or monitor your daily habits. You're reinforcing your way of living as an integrated day-to-day experience—not as a series of random events. You'll be carving out "quality time" for the simple activities that make the rest of your life work more effectively.

After you've been regularly practicing the Daily Solo and Journal, you'll find it has become a part of you. You'll also find yourself taking spontaneous "mini-solos" during your day. These mini-solos (one to two minutes) can be taken at any time. If you feel stressed or wish to focus on a situation, simply go quickly through the eight steps. Then take a deep breath and move back into your day.

Through the Daily Solo, you'll find that your mind can be your best friend on the road to an enhanced quality of life. You'll have cultivated the reflective skills that are so important to coping with life and to your personal growth.

Selected References

Armstrong, Thomas. *7 Kinds of Smart*. Los Angeles: Tarcher, 1993.

Bardwick, Judith. *The Plateauing Trap*. New York: Amacom, 1986.

Bennis, Warren, and Nanus, Burt. Leaders: *The Strategies for Taking Charge*. New York: Harper & Row, 1985.

Bolles, Richard N. *The Three Boxes of Life*. Berkeley, CA: Ten Speed Press, 1978.

——. *What Color Is Your Parachute?* Berkeley, CA: Ten Speed Press, 1993.

Bridges, William. *Transitions*. Reading, MA: Addison-Wesley, 1980.

Campbell, David. *If You Don't Know Where You're Going, You'll Probably End Up Somewhere Else*. Niles, IL: Argus, 1974.

Campbell, Joseph. *The Power of Myth*. New York: Doubleday, 1988.

Cousins, Norman. *Anatomy of an Illness*. New York: Bantam, 1978.

Dychtwald, Ken. *Age Wave*. Los Angeles: Tarcher, 1989.

Elgin, Duane. *Voluntary Simplicity*. New York: William Morrow, 1981.

Eyre, Linda, and Eyre, Richard. *Life Balance*. New York: Ballantine, 1987.

Frankl, Viktor. *Man's Search for Meaning*. New York: Pocket Books, 1963.

Gardner, John. *Self-Renewal*. New York: Harper & Row, 1981.

Gawain, Shakti. *Creative Visualization*. Mill Valley, CA: Whatever Publishing, 1978.

Hagberg, Janet. *Real Power*. San Francisco: Harper & Row, 1984.

Hagberg, Janet, and Leider, Richard. *The Inventurers: Excursions in Life and Career Renewal*. Reading, MA: Addison-Wesley, 1988.

Hopson, Barrie, and Scally, Mike. *Assertiveness*. San Diego: Pfeiffer & Company, 1983.

——. *Build Your Own Rainbow*. San Diego: Pfeiffer & Company, 1993.

Kushner, Harold. *When All You've Ever Wanted Isn't Enough*. New York: Summit, 1986.

LaBier, Douglas. *Modern Madness*. Reading, MA: Addison-Wesley, 1986.

Larson, Roland, and Larson, Doris. *I Need to Have You Know Me*. San Francisco: Harper, 1980.

Leider, Richard J. *The Power of Purpose*. New York: Fawcett, 1985.

McNally, David. *Even Eagles Need a Push*. San Francisco: Trans-Form, 1990.

Naisbitt, John, and Aburdene, Patricia. *Megatrends Two Thousand*. New York: William Morrow, 1989.

Nouwen, Henri J.M. *Out of Solitude*. Notre Dame, IN: Ave Maria Press, 1974.

Paulus, Trina. *Hope for the Flowers*. New York: Paulist Press, 1972.

Peck, M. Scott. *The Road Less Traveled*. New York: Simon & Schuster, 1978.

Robinson, Bryan. *Work Addiction*. Deerfield, FL: Health Communications, 1989.

Ryan, Regina Sara, and Travis, John W. *Wellness Workbook: A Guide to Attaining a High Level of Wellness*. Berkeley, CA: Ten Speed Press, 1981.

Smith, Maggie. *Changing Course*. San Diego: Pfeiffer & Company, 1993.

Wilson, Larry. *Changing the Game*. New York: Simon & Schuster, 1987.

Winston, Stephanie. *The Organized Executive*. New York: Warner, 1983.

Woodward, Harry, and Buchholz, Steve. *Aftershock*. New York: Wiley, 1989.

Index

Editor:

JoAnn Padgett

Editorial Assistants:

Heidi Erika Callinan

Katharine Pechtimaldjian

Cover:

Tom Lewis, Inc.

Interior Layout:

Frank E. Schiele

Photographs:

Charles St. John